THE YOUTH TRUTH

Coaching & Parenting
in Today's Crazy Youth Sports World

- *Build Unshakeable Confidence*
- *Rekindle Joy & Passion*
- *Develop Successful Leaders*

BY ANDREW SIMPSON

This book is dedicated to my dad, Kevin Simpson. Dad, you were the ultimate sports parent. Thank you for always *showing up.*
For being at every game, no matter what. For never yelling and for always supporting. Jack may not have met you in this lifetime, but he *will* know how amazing you really were. I know you would be proud of this book. I can see the smile on your face and can hear your response now: "Great job, bud."

TABLE OF CONTENTS

Introduction 1

Part 1: Shining the Spotlight on the Current State of Our Youth

Chapter 1: The Silent Killer of Your Athletes' Performance 37

Chapter 2: Injuries are at an All-Time High 41

Chapter 3: The Paradox of Year-Round Sports................................. 43

Chapter 4: Solutions to the Injury Epidemic.................................... 45

Chapter 5: Owning Your Fight.. 51

Chapter 6: Where Has Our Current Paradigm Gotten Us? 55

Chapter 7: The Problems Defined.. 59

Chapter 8: Don't Give Your Athletes the Wrong Medicine 65

Chapter 9: Shadows Without Substance 67

Chapter 10: A New Approach 69

Part 2: Love-Powered Coaching Principles

Chapter 11: What does Love Require of me? 75

Chapter 12: The Coaching Shift.. 79

Chapter 13: Going Deep to Ignite CHANGE 83

Chapter 14: Love-Powered Coaching.. 87

Chapter 15: A Life-Transforming Coach 111

Chapter 16: Equipping and Empowering... 115

Chapter 17: Stand in the Gap, Change a Life 119

Chapter 18: The Two Most Powerful Words: "Coach Says" 123

Chapter 19: If Not You, Who? 127

Chapter 20: Fun, Love and Inspiration:
           The Foundation for Unstoppable Growth 131

Part 3: Training the Mind

Chapter 21: Mindset Matters More.. 141

Chapter 22: Unlocking Limitless Potential..................................... 153

Chapter 23: The Personal Power of Written Introspection 159

Chapter 24: Bad Questions → Bad Answers →
           REALLY Bad Decisions 167

Chapter 25: Self-Worth: The Foundation of Confidence 171

Chapter 26: Becoming Unshakeable(ish) 177

Chapter 27: Blink and Sports are Gone 187

Chapter 28: Leading Through Chaos.. 195

Chapter 29: Tough Decisions are Long-Term Investments............ 199

Chapter 30: More Important Than SUCCESS Is............................ 203

Chapter 31: Stand Out to Be Outstanding..................................... 209

Part 4: Putting it Into Practice

Game-Ready Mental Preparedness... 217

       Lesson 1: The Mistake Ritual 219

       Lesson 2: The U-Curve.. 223

       Lesson 3: How the BEST Operate "Between Points"......... 225

       Lesson 4: Overcoming Self-Doubts
                by Reframing Your Thoughts............................. 229

Lesson 5: Energy and Enthusiasm: Two Secret
        Ingredients to Gain the Mental Edge 233
Lesson 6: Acting Medium 237
Lesson 7: Getting OUT of Your head and INTO The Zone 241

Life-Ready Mental Preparedness 249

Life Ready Exercise 1: CORE VALUES 254
Life Ready Exercise 2: Role Models. 258
Life Ready Exercise 3: Strengths, Gifts, and Talents
                    that Last 264
Life Ready Exercise 4: Confidence 269

Exercises for the Coach 281

Lesson #1: Root Before Fruit, ALWAYS! 281
Lesson #2: Creating Your Team Theme 283
Lesson #3: Next Level: Hone your How 284
Lesson #4: Defining your Performance Pillars 287
Lesson #5: Communicate to Connect 289
Lesson #6: Getting Your Athletes Out of Their Heads 291
Lesson #7: The Cup, The Sleeve, The Napkin 299

Conclusion 303
About the Author 305
Acknowledgements 309

INTRODUCTION

"**W**HAT ARE YOU DOING??? WHAT WERE YOU THINKING??? COME ON BRANDON, THAT WAS A TERRIBLE DECISION! LET'S GO!!" screamed the "coach."

It was the winter of 2009. I was 19 years old, working at the front desk of an indoor sports complex. One particular night after a work shift, I felt oddly compelled to venture over to watch a soccer game.

Normally after a shift at work, I would sprint to my car to get on with my night. This particular night, God had different plans for me. Within minutes of setting foot into the stands, I heard that horrifying sound that made the hairs on my neck stand up. It was the blood-curdling scream of an insecure sports coach whose priorities were out of whack. I knew in that moment that there was a problem.

This was a recreational soccer game – for nine-year-olds!

The Problem

A young lady walked into our gym one night, prepared to do her workout. She seemed off, but it was just "normal teen behavior."

After the warm-up, she grabbed her workout program and began to do her first set of exercises. It was not long before one of our coaches noticed something concerning.

She had marks on her forearm.

Our coach quickly came to me. "Andrew, something is wrong. It looks like she's been cutting herself. What do we do?"

Come to find out, for months this track star had been cutting herself in an attempt to ease her pain.

Think about this for a minute. In track, arms are exposed *all the time*. No one noticed, likely because everyone from the coaches to her teammates was very *busy* – busy trying to win, busy trying to be successful.

This young lady was noticeably sad more days than not, if you *really* looked at her. She always replied, "Fine, I guess" when asked the question, "How's track going?"

Immediately, I brought her into my office. I sat down with her and told her I noticed she seemed off (I did not call her out for the marks on her arms). I simply wanted to give her the opportunity to vent.

The pressure, the expectations from coaches, and the fear of disappointing her parents was so real. *"The only way my mom will be proud of me is if I qualify for the state meet. Then I will need to earn a D1 college scholarship. Then she might be proud."*

Eventually, without me even probing, she told me she had been cutting herself and showed me her forearms. I tried not to overreact, as this is the quickest way to get your students to never open up to you again.

That night, I called her parents to let them know what we had discovered. Thankfully this opened up conversations on how to lessen the pressure that their daughter was feeling from them.

We continued to work with the young lady two times per week with an emphasis on making her training experience fun and enjoyable, while also facilitating good discussions that allowed her to continue to open up to us. We wanted her to realize that we really did care about her as a person, not just an athlete.

Take a quick survey right now of the athletes you coach or parent. *Do you know with absolute certainty that they are mentally and emotionally healthy? Do they believe you care about them MORE as a person than you do about their athletic success?* If they are not opening up to you and coming to *you* for guidance and mentorship, this may be why.

This story simply illustrates another big challenge we are facing today as youth influencers:

We are Blinded by Performance

We are so focused on our athletes' athletic needs that we cannot even see beyond the physical challenges. We are so dialed into helping them on the field that we forget to help them as a person.

Pause for a moment. Wasn't it the coach who took an interest in your *personal life* that really transformed you? *That* was the coach you happily gave your best effort to *on the field.*

Fast forward about two years, and this young lady is now breaking records at her school and has many colleges pursuing her. She is training fiercely at the gym, lifting more weight, and moving faster than ever before. She's a beast.

But perhaps most importantly, she is smiling a lot more, her relationship with her mom and dad is whole, her grades are up, and her friendships are thriving.

What I get the most joy from is knowing that this young lady is now one of the few student-athletes nowadays who achieve joy *and* peak performance without sacrificing relationships, mental health, emotional health, or physical well-being. She has balance and is succeeding in all aspects of life. Throughout this book, I am so excited to share with you the formula that is guaranteed to help your athletes achieve the same type of balance and results.

When you focus on the root, the fruit will come. This is a fundamental concept of love-powered leadership that we will explore deeper in part four of this book.

The Problem Ignored

"When a problem goes unaddressed or unnoticed, the results can be devastating. But it is far worse when there is a problem and the professionals who can fix it refuse to acknowledge that it exists."
– ANONYMOUS

I am not a traditional sports coach. I work in the fitness and sports performance side of athletics. However, I do get to work with more than 150 different athletes a week, which gives me a unique opportunity that most sports coaches do not have. I've noticed that fewer kids than ever are genuinely excited about their sport, while more kids than ever are experiencing stress, anxiety, overwhelm, burnout, and chronic overuse injuries. When joy is low and anxiety is high, high performance on the field is not sustainable, and neither is mental or emotional stability.

There are problems going on with our kids today, and coaches and parents all over the world are ignoring it – *normalizing it*. The first part of this book highlights the problems, but the rest is about proven solutions.

So what are the problems? I am sure you could name a few. One obvious one is how worked up parents and coaches get over a game.

Fist fighting at youth athletic events is a new hobby for some. The adults are feeling more anxious for their kids during games than the kids are. We value scholarships over relationships, club sports practices over church, and the list goes on and on. Is this normal?

- Four-hour practices after school. Priorities.
- Six games in a weekend. Priorities.
- $5000 a year on club sports. Priorities.
- Quality conversations at dinner replaced with critiques about the game. Priorities.
- Every family vacation dictated by the next tournament. Priorities.
- Spending 12 hours a week on sports performance enhancement but no time to train the mind and heart? Priorities.

I want to share a better way to lead your kids to greatness. To inspire and motivate them in a way that leads to unparalleled, lifelong success. As we go through this journey together, please do not misunderstand the Youth Truth message. I don't condemn anyone for valuing sports. I like sports too. I operate a youth athletic development business. The problem isn't that we like sports. The problem is that many of us are *exalting sports without even realizing the damage it is causing, as well as the opportunity costs.*

There is a better way to help your students maximize athletic potential *and* achieve balance and success in all of life's most important arenas. By picking up this book and carving out the time to read it I know with absolute certainty that you care about your legacy and have a burning desire to be a better leader.

If the goal is to produce beasts on the field no matter what the expense, then those *means* I listed above might get your athletes there (that is, if they do not get injured or burn out and quit before then).

However, if your primary goal is to see your kids truly happy, successful, injury free, mentally and emotionally healthy, self-disciplined, driven by values and strong priorities...then I suggest you keep reading so we can forge a new path that will ultimately result in a better performing athlete on the field.

Sports used to be a vehicle to a higher performing young man or woman. They used to be a sure path to see your kid become more confident, courageous, a better teammate, a leader, and more successful.

Today, as you will see throughout part one of this book, "The State of Our Youth," sports are causing more harm than good. If we would just look past the immediate impact of our decisions with our athletes, if we could see the future, the long-term implications, we would surely get off the path we are currently on and choose a new one.

I've seen enough, and so have you. This book is the first step in my mission to link arms with *you*, the youth influencer, to spread what I call The Love-Powered Leadership Movement.

It is all about strengthening the minds, winning the hearts, and inspiring the souls of your athletes.

As you read this book allow the words to ignite hope, confidence, and faith that you ARE the solution. You *can* help every single one of your students transform their mindset and step into lives of confidence, purpose, and success.

The methods I share in the pages that follow have helped thousands of kids unlock their true capacity. I believe that together we can impact millions.

We Hold These Truths to Be Self-Evident

Thomas Jefferson wrote those famous words in the Declaration of Independence in 1776. He spoke of the things that he, along with the Founding Fathers, found to be self-evident – or in other words, the things that were *obvious: not needing to be explained or demonstrated.* Based on human observation, Jefferson found that these were things were indeed factual. They were proven based on observational evidence.

I have found *these* statements to be self-evident:

1. There are gigantic problems going on in youth sports today.

2. Parents are getting crazier, more obsessed, and their actions are resulting in kids with less confidence, more fear, and more self-doubt (few knowingly, most unknowingly).

3. Coaches are having trouble *connecting* with the new generations. We are gravitating to tactics and tricks rather than using time-tested principles to influence. *The quickest way to change a kid's mind is to connect with his or her heart.* In part two I will share with you the simplest, most effective way to increase your influence with your athletes tenfold.

4. Injuries from overuse are at an all-time-high and will continue to rise if we do not shift our priorities and values as coaches and parents.

5. Most coaches are not aware of (or are not effectively leveraging) their immense power.

6. Our obsession with *outcomes*, which comes from *selfish ambition*, is leading to *dozens* of other problems and keeping our kids from the actual outcomes they desire!

7. Some of those problems showing up in our youth include:

    a. Comparison, jealousy, envy, and greed

    b. Fear of failure, people pleaser syndrome caused by fear of disappointing, fear of rejection, fear of falling behind

    c. Microwave mentality (that is, instant gratification), lack of stick-to-it-iveness (the ability to stay focused and grind it out)

8. If the youth influencers of the world do not rise up to change the standards of leadership, the state of our youth will continue to experience the fall: low ambition and drive, more anxiety, more depression, and more outward acts of an inward struggle, such as suicide.

9. The solutions to all of this are obvious but under-practiced because of two things: incompetency and conformity – not knowing what to do and choosing to follow the crowds to destruction.

The Truth

Few athletes are achieving peak performance *consistently*. Most are mentally drained and stressed. Every week I hear kids say, "I'm so stressed." They are not being mentored for life, but rather *trained* and instructed to be better at a *finite game*.

It's rare that I come across a kid who knows what it means to be a leader, the very thing our world is in desperate need of right now. Instead, they are learning how to look out for "number one" and seek self-promotion through social media.

The list goes on. Despite the fact that more athletes are experiencing overuse injuries than ever before, most coaches and parents are avoiding the proactive work of increasing recovery time and injury prevention practices, which in some cases include the things so many of us fear – time off and shorter (but better) practices!

We need to start this journey by imagining a future for our youth that is far better than anything we ever had for ourselves.

I IMAGINE

I want to share with you one of my *favorite* exercises. I do it for my family, my finances, my career, and in this case, my purpose in life which is to impact millions of kids, coaches, and parents all over the world.

Inspiration Exercise: "I imagine…"

What do I imagine?

"I imagine a world where every kid has a mentor leader. A humble coach with integrity, who loves them unconditionally, mentors them, inspires them, and challenges them to be their best.

I imagine **hundreds of thousands** *of coaches all over the world coming together as a community to spread love-powered leadership all over the sports landscape.*

I imagine our student-athletes experiencing so much joy playing sports that they desire to continue sports long after organized athletics are over.

I imagine a world in which coaches and parents are supportive but refrain from crossing the "overbearing line".

I imagine a world where kids, coaches, and parents are so **secure** *and* **confident** *that they do not need accomplishments, scholarships, power, or applause in order to feel worthy or fulfilled. They know who* *they are and why they matter and feel no desire to compare themselves to others.*

I imagine a world where every young man and woman discovers their unique gifts, passions, and strengths, and eventually goes on to lead a purpose-driven life.

I imagine a sports industry that God is pleased with, one that honors Him and values things that matter 10 years from now over the ones that wither away 10 minutes from now.

I imagine a world where parents and coaches value who their kids become over what they accomplish.

*I imagine a world where spiritual, mental, and emotional fitness becomes a priority, knowing that this approach does indeed lead to peak **physical** performance.*

Oh how I imagine a better world for our youth.

*I imagine confident, strong, authentic, courageous young men and women. Generations **WILL** be changed. It **WILL** be awesome."*

Everything starts with **imagination**. A **dream**. A **vision**. That is mine. What's yours? Make sure to write it. As the Bible says, "Where there is no vision, the people perish."

Exercise Idea:

For my family, I imagine...

For my finances, I imagine...

For my child's athletics, I imagine...

For my child's academics, I imagine...

For my future health (spiritual, emotional, mental, physical) I imagine...

Keep going. You cannot be what you cannot see. Engage in this exercise; it could change your life, and consequently, the kids you influence.

Before we get into the meat and potatoes, I need to share with you my story, not because I am comfortable sharing this stuff, but because in many ways, this story has shaped my motives and philosophies as a coach.

My Story

On March 30, 2018, my life changed.

My family was finally becoming "normal." More stable. More *functional.*

For the past 15 years, there had been significant, non-stop dysfunction in my family. I know every family goes through stuff. God prepares us and even *assures* us that we *all* will go through stuff. I find it odd when people say things like, "I can't believe God would let that happen!" The fact is that He told us it would. God said, "In this world you will have trouble." That's pretty clear.

> **Note**: If you do not believe what I believe, that's OK. We can respect one another without agreeing. The principles I share in this book work *no matter what one believes.* In a spirit of authenticity and "realness," I decided that the right thing to do was to share who I really am and *why* I coach the way I do. I do share my foundation of faith throughout the book and kindly ask for you to respect my views and recognize that in no way am I trying to push them onto you.

To save you the entire Simpson Family Saga, I'll just share the biggest obstacles that impacted my future.

Both of my sisters were addicted to heroin and alcohol. It was bad. As a result, my parents' marriage was turned upside down on multiple occasions. The dysfunction really began when I was in middle school.

My oldest sister battled addiction for more than 15 years. I remember the police being at our house far too often. There were many nights spent looking for her, rescuing her, wondering if she was alive. You can imagine the wear and tear on our family over a decade and a half.

Just when my older sister finally got sober for good in 2017, we found out that my younger sister had been using heroin for the past four years and was at rock bottom. I remember the feeling in my stomach when my older sister charged into PFP one afternoon, pushed me into my office, and told me that my little sister was addicted to one of the most dangerous drugs on the planet.

> **Note:** I'll reference PFP often in this book. It stands for Player's Fitness & Performance. It is the youth transformation and athletic development business that I founded in 2014.

I had no clue. I was so busy getting married, moving, building a business, and trying to change the world that I didn't even know my baby sister was hanging onto her life by a thread. There is a lesson for all of us there: stop being too busy to notice the status of your loved ones' hearts. By the grace of God, my sister hung on. She rose from the ashes just as my older sister had done a year before.

It brings tears to my eyes just thinking about my sisters and the amazing place God has them in today. It's awesome. They are on fire, leading purpose driven lives.

In 2018, my parents were finally about to experience the season of *calm* that had eluded them for the past 15 years – a season where they could enjoy one another.

In March, my dad took his final international business trip of his career. He was done traveling. He was so excited to step into the next chapter with his bride of the past 32 years. He had two young grandchildren, three healthy children, and a daughter-in-law he considered his own.

Prior to leaving for that last trip, my dad had been complaining of neck and shoulder pain. He had been coming to the gym for the past year. One of his goals was to loosen up and become more flexible. Mobility would surely add quality to his life seeing as how his upper body was so stiff that it caused him to have trouble taking full breaths. And since you take 18,000-22,000 breaths a day, it is pretty important that you are able to take good ones. It seemed like we were making progress.

Despite the neck and shoulder pain, my dad was doing perfect chinups, pushups, lunges, and squats with almost 50% of his body weight at age 60. He was eating clean, he had stopped smoking five years prior, and he was doing his best to become healthier and fitter than he had ever been.

But the neck pain was too rough to ignore. Isn't it unfortunate that physical pain can be so debilitating? The presence of pain will often keep you from pursuing *gain* in other areas of your life. It is said that when you *have* your physical health you have a thousand dreams, but when you do not have your health, you have only *one* dream.

Chiropractors, massage therapists, physical therapists, breathing techniques – we did it all. No relief.

Finally, an MRI was ordered. What was it? Muscle spasms? A strain? Hopefully not a herniated disc.

On March 30, 2018, he received the following news from his doctor: "Kevin, you have a large mass on your lung. We need you to come in immediately to run tests."

After a biopsy, PET scan, brain scan, and many other tests, he received the results.

Stage IV lung cancer.

He called me when I was in MOM's organic market shopping. He murmured the unclear words, "Stage IV... in my bones, I think... I don't know, bud... can't really remember what they said."

I knelt on the floor of the grocery store for what seemed like hours. I can't explain the feeling, I just know I hated that moment. I have extremely high levels of what many would call "realistic optimism." I knew God had not retired from doing miracles. I knew cancer had been beaten many times before. But when you find out your dad has one of the worst kinds, you can literally feel the devil trying to fill your soul with doubt and hopelessness. I knelt down on that cold, hard floor in disbelief. I prayed.

The cancer was in his lungs, liver, spine, bones, and brain, and they needed to begin radiation immediately.

Over the next seven months, alongside my wife, sisters, and mother, I witnessed the most awful, gut-wrenching, painful battle I've ever seen or ever want to see again. I want to give you a quick back story about my dad.

He was cool -- way cooler than me. He drove motorcycles. He had cool tattoos. He had a pet rat when he was a kid. He was the handiest of handymen. He worked on cars and could fix *anything*.

I did not tell him this nearly enough, but I looked up to him. I admired him, not for anything he *did*, but for who he *was*. He was so good on the inside.

He was kind, non-judgmental, and authentic. Everyone who met him said he had a light that radiated from him. There was a special humility about him that not everyone has. Someone once told me that humility is a realistic view of one's importance. My dad had that. He was a "meek man", something I aspire to have written on my gravestone someday.

My dad spoke to a poor person the same way he spoke to a rich man. He chose to hang with people from all walks of life. He said hi to everyone. He got along with everyone. I never remember seeing him buy something or do something just because he saw someone else do it. I don't think he did it on purpose, but he never conformed to societal norms. He lived Romans 12:2 without even knowing it. He was *quietly confident.* He never tried to be someone he was not. And dad *always, always, always* showed up.

I remember this one basketball game when I was a junior in high school. It was 20 minutes before tipoff, and a family friend approached me on the sidelines. "Andrew, your dad just called. He was in a motorcycle accident on Horine Road. He tried to avoid a deer and ended up laying the bike down. He is ok. He wanted me to let you know he is on his way but may be a few minutes late."

That was my dad. He loved my mom and us three kids more than anything. And that love was unconditional, meaning we did not have to act a certain way, perform to a certain standard, or achieve a certain grade in order to receive his love.

He was always in the stands *quietly cheering me on*. He never criticized or condemned my performance, but always had an open mind and open ear *if* I wanted to talk about my play.

For a while, I did not understand how he did this *without* being hyper-intentional about it! How did he avoid the pitfalls of being an overbearing sports parent? How did he refrain from the post-game criticisms? How did he find the perfect blend of encouragement and love? I now know that it was that status of his *heart.*

The status of his *heart* determined what he believed about the importance of sports. He knew sports mattered some, but not *most.* He did not have expectations for my performance. Not only did he *desire* for me to enjoy the game and learn life lessons, but his actions backed those desires.

What a lesson. I want to be like him as a dad and as a sports parent. He did not do it on purpose, but rather because of who he was on the inside. Want to be a better coach or parent? Work on what is on the *inside.* My dad was an awesome sports dad.

I wish I could say the story ended with my dad surviving, that God provided one of His miracles. I wish I could say that my dad made it to see the birth of my first child (my wife found out she was pregnant just days after my dad's diagnosis).

Just seven months after diagnosis, my dad went to paradise to "chill," as he would say. This book is a tribute to my loving, earthly father, Kevin Simpson, who fought tooth and nail for his life, for his family. Cancer won the battle, but my dad won the war. He's in Heaven. If you've lost someone to cancer, my heart aches with you. It's not a glorious way for a person to leave this world; however, your pain is not meaningless. Like me, on any given day you probably pass at least one person who is going through what you went through. And you are now relatable in a way you never were before. Use your pain for another's gain. While you will never stop missing that person, choosing this way helps the healing process and the example will shine onto the kids you lead as well.

Time Capsules

One reason I share his story in this book is because I wish my dad would have left me some special things in a time capsule – videos of him talking to me and my future children, letters, journals, maybe a book. He did not, but now I have that opportunity.

Too many of us are living as if we will never die. I agree with Erwin McManus, an amazing pastor and author of the best-selling book *The Last Arrow*, who said this:

> *"What will give someone solace or haunt them until their final breath is what they could have done but did not, who they could have been but never became, the life they could have lived that never came to life."*

As I mentioned already, I was not eager, nor did I feel ready to write this book. I thought I needed to learn more, coach more, fail more, and experience more *first*. I thought I needed some more *confidence* before writing this book. How ironic, since a big part of this book is how to help kids become more confident. I've learned that being *ready* is simply a state of mind.

And then, on the morning of November 30, 2018, just two weeks after my dad passed away, I read something written by Mark Batterson, author of the best-selling book, *Chase the Lion*.

He said that the reason he writes books is because books are like time capsules. He wants his great-great-grandchildren to know what he *lived* for and what he was willing to *die* for.

I have something to live for. I also have something I would die for. Just like you, I have an ache in my soul to *see* change happen. We all have something that pains us on the inside when we *see* it out of place and messed up on the outside. The only difference in the way I operate now is that I no longer *long to see change happen.* I am committed to *making* it happen. I now try to live by the saying, *Ready, FIRE, Aim.*

Procrastination and fear will paralyze you from making the change that you were destined to make.

What is this book really about?

The Youth Truth contains an unpopular message. If it was popular, it wouldn't need to be shared. But for the past five years, I have let the fear of rejection keep me quiet. I have kept this message bottled up in my heart and mind, and as a result, have kept the impact limited to those in our ZIP code.

"Andrew is soft. His team cares about all that *love stuff.* They don't build real athletes; they think everyone deserves a participation trophy." These were the painful responses I built up in my mind that would surely come from critics who may hear *The Youth Truth* message.

Despite the words of affirmation I receive weekly, I still cowered in fear. I had a high acceptance rate with the people who read the emails, and I didn't want to mess it up and receive criticism by being bold and outspoken.

That is, until now. You see, I've learned that the point of life isn't to get people to agree with you. The point of life is not to say and do things that are accepted by everyone. That is actually a path that leads to a comfortable life of regret.

The point of life is to connect with your Creator, find out why He put you on this earth, and then to use your gifts and your voice to fulfill the assignments He gives you (by the way, He has much bigger assignments for you and He is eager to reveal them to you as you boldly and courageously step up). Ultimately, you are here to make your dent in the world, to leave it better than you found it, and to hear the words, "Well done, good and faithful servant." This will require the courage to move forward even when it isn't popular.

My team and I define success this way. Based on that definition, we are on the right track. We have already begun to see the kids we work with go on to become young men and women who are purpose-driven leaders who are driven to make an impact.

If you are the kind of coach that checks their ego at the door daily and has a burning desire to see the students you work with become who they were created to become, then *you* are my tribe.

I know that through us, God wants to do some of his most important work. Our effectiveness as coach is not limited by our potential, but rather it is *limitless* based on the true capacity we have when we lay down our agents and allow God to be God.

There is a movement happening right now–a movement being executed by coaches who are brave enough to take responsibility for repairing the broken youth sports industry. It is open to any coach or youth influencer who wants to step up and embrace the challenge. Will you join me?

Is the youth sports industry REALLY broken?

In June of 2019, the headline from CBS in Lakewood, Colorado read:

PARENTS BEHAVING BADLY: Violent Brawl Breaks Out at Little League Game For 7-Year-Olds

You can YouTube this. It was *bad*. Parents were hospitalized with critical injuries. What those kids saw, they can never unsee. And for the developing brain of a seven-year-old, the damage could be tragic down the road.

This is not the first (nor will it be the last) brawl that breaks out at a youth sports game. There are literally dozens of these that happen every year. But even *one* per year, in my opinion, is proof that the sports industry is broken.

It is broken, but not beyond repair. As leadership expert John Maxwell tells us, "Everything rises and falls on leadership."

Nations, businesses, families, and churches all rise and fall on leadership. And guess what? Youth sports organizations are no exception. Youth fitness businesses are no exception. You show me a *great* team, I'll show you a great coach. You show me a world-class youth sports organization built on good morals and values, I will show you a great leader who dreamed it and great leaders who are running it every day.

WHO ARE THE LEADERS OF YOUR TEAM? Who is leading your organization? Who is leading your kids? Who is leading the parents?

YOU ARE! You have the power. You can turn the ship around. It's not too late. As long as we don't lose hope, faith, or grit, we can change this industry. But we have to take responsibility for the bad and we have to *give away* credit for the good that happens. That is what great leaders do. You cannot do it alone, and neither can I. We need to lead with love. We need to lead well. We need to change the game. It starts with what we *believe*.

What do I BELIEVE About My Purpose?

For the first six years of my coaching career, I *believed* I was a strength and conditioning coach. Therefore, I *thought* of myself as one who is responsible for helping athletes get strong, fast, and "tough." For the past four years and counting, thanks to the myriad mistakes I made combined with discovering my life's purpose, I now *believe* I am a Life Transforming Coach and a Mentor-Leader who was created to build confident, successful, servant-leaders. I also *believe* that I am called to multiply that impact by leading other coaches and parents who share similar desires to positively influence kids all over the world.

I now *think* of myself completely differently because of what I *believe* about my purpose. I think of myself as a conduit through whom God works to help athletes transform from the inside out. And because I *think* of myself and my responsibilities in this way now, my *actions* and *habits* as a coach are completely different.

My priorities and motives have changed. If I have one hour to coach an athlete, I better use that time wisely. Spending 58 minutes on skills, drills, and conditioning, and two minutes on their confidence and mindset does not seem like a good allocation of time for a coach who wants to make a lifelong impact.

If you *believe* that you are a "baseball coach" or a "strength coach," this book will challenge you to view yourself as *more* so that you can impact your athletes more deeply. Who we *believe* we are determines our identity and the way we think about our *responsibilities*.

Beliefs (which reside in your heart) → Thoughts (which reside in your mind) → Feelings → Actions → Habits → Results

Who do you believe you really are? Who do you believe you have the power to be? *Believe* in your heart you can be more, and you will do more and accomplish more (results). *Believe* you can change lives. *Believe* you can positively affect generations.

> *"For as he thinketh in his heart, so he is."*
> PROVERBS 23:7

The Movement

Joe and Samantha bring their son and daughter to work out with us at PFP. Their kids are hands down the best leaders, the best communicators, the most respectful, the most coachable, and the most compassionate brother and sister I have ever met. They are both exceptional athletes. They come up to each one of our coaches after training sessions with a big smile, they shake our hands, and say thank you. And it is authentic. One day I asked them who their greatest coach in their life was, and they both replied, "My mom and dad."

"Who am I not being that my players' eyes are not shining?"

What this quote really means is, "Why might my example as a leader be unattractive? Why don't my players look at *me* as a leader and automatically have a burning desire to be a leader as well?" Leadership *should* be so attractive that your kids can't help but to want to be one. This was a defining moment for me as a leader.

As Dave Ramsey so eloquently puts it, "As the leader, you are both the problem with your organization (or family, or team) *and* the solution."

If you learn to embrace these tough questions and do your best to try to *unpack them*, as opposed to getting offended and resenting them, your leadership and influence will be amplified. Coachability starts with the leader.

This one question made me realize that it was time to be a real, authentic, vulnerable leader for my team and my athletes. I decided to tear the walls down and let them know where I had failed. I shared with them my insecurities about leading them well. I shared with them that I was not living in alignment with my values. And because of my poor example of leadership, *my player's eyes were not shining.*

Do you want to know the encouraging ending? As a result of me looking in the mirror and realizing *I* was the problem, and then communicating that openly, my team trusted and looked up to me *more.* It's crazy how this leadership thing works.

Who is this book for?

This book is designed for three populations: coaches, parents, and student-athletes.

1) Legacy Coaches

This book is for the coach who wants to become the coach they always wish they had.

It is for the coach who is committed to getting better everyday and recognizes that he or she can learn from anyone. If you have ever struggled to motivate or inspire your athletes to action, this book will give you the tools you need.

Maybe you are a coach like me who has never learned how to implement "mindset coaching". Part four contains dozens of exercises that will help your athletes win the mental game.

Maybe you just want to connect with your player's hearts and have a deeper, more meaningful impact in their lives. The principles in this book will help you to relate .

2) The Parent

This book is also for the sports parent who is ready to do whatever it takes to see their son or daughter be happy, successful, and confident.

Maybe you want to improve your connection and influence with your athlete and learn more about what is truly going on in their minds.

I think sports parenting in today's world may be the toughest job. Whether you are the parent who has recently become aware that you get way too worked up about sports and you want to change, or you are the parent who can't stand the parents who get way too worked up, this book will be eye-opening and helpful for you.

Another challenge I know many parents have is communication.

"What do I say to them after a game? Before a game?"

I will share very practical tips throughout the book. After all, as a parent, you can only control what you can control. I commend you for picking up this book. It is rare to find forward-thinking parents who care about avoiding the pitfalls that many experience.

3) The Athlete

The philosophies and exercises in this book will help the student-athletes who are struggling with confidence, low self-esteem, comparison, and self-doubt. This book will fill them up with confidence and will help them to navigate the rocky terrains of middle school, high school, and college.

This book will also help the advanced athletes who seem to have it all together, the ones who are rock stars on and off the field, committed to D1 programs, straight-A students, and socially thriving. These are the kids who can benefit from the mental preparation and leadership sections of this book.

Writing Creates Clarity

Over the past ten years the self-discovery and clarity that has come from doing introspective writing exercises, facilitated by a coach, has literally changed my life and the lives of millions of people around the world.

Three years ago I realized that those same writing and mindset exercises had the potential to change the lives of 12-year-olds, 15-year-olds, 20-year-olds, and every other school-aged kid who took the time to sit down, think, and write. I challenge you right now to validate that claim. Spend five minutes right now answering the following question with pen and paper:

At the end of my life, what are the 3 questions I am going to ask myself to evaluate if I lived a purpose driven, meaningful life?

For me, I say it is going to be these three:

1. Did I love others the way Jesus loves me?

2. Did I fully unleash and maximize the gifts God gave me, or did I hold back?

3. Did I lead teams, missions, and causes that will last long after I am gone? Did my leadership leave ripples?

What do you believe YOUR three questions will be?

1. _____

2. _____

3. _____

Was I right? When you ask the right questions and spend enough quality time thinking through them, the breakthroughs are monumental.

What I found interesting back in 2016 was that the teenage and college-age students I worked with *craved* this type of stuff. I thought they would hate it, but they loved it. Not every exercise, not every kid, and not every time, but it was definitely an overall *positive* addition to my coaching.

The idea of having a mentor-leader guide them through the obstacles of their lives, as well as to help them identify the true path to their best self, was attractive to them. And when I was vulnerable and shared my answers, failures, dreams, and desires, they liked it even more. I became more relatable. I have found that student-athletes across the board need this type of coaching more than the extra reps hitting off the tee. It leads to trust between you and your athletes. It leads to more influence. It leads to a kids' life transformed. You will see in Section 4.

I was wrong when I wrote off the idea that "mindset coaching" would be worth the time and effort on my part. I was wrong to knock something before trying it. Doesn't every parent hate when their kids claim that green-colored foods are nasty before even trying them?

The fact is that we live in the age of anxiety and "youth stress" (which really wasn't a thing even 10-15 years ago). There is massive comparison going on and your kids are lacking clarity about who they are or if they even matter. There is so much noise and only being *still* can really help it. Of course kids want this stuff. But more importantly, they *need* it in order to accomplish what you want them to on the field.

Every race car driver knows that performance on the outside is unsustainable when things are broken on the inside. Until now, coaches have just never offered life coaching to kids before in such a way that they can relate to and connect with. We now know that our youth population is craving this type of training right now.

I do not love the term "life coaching," so throughout this book I refer to it as "mindset coaching." It is essentially high-performance mentoring for the mental edge in sports and life.

Be aware, the type of training we are about to subject you to is uncommon. But guess what? The results you and your athletes experience will be uncommon as well.

Success, Significance, or Something Different?

"What's your why, Coach?"

If you are a coach in your twenties, this part may be all you need to read. If you are a veteran coach this will either help *you* or it will be transformational for the coaches you are bringing up underneath you.

Over the past ten years I have gone through three "phases" as a coach. I believe I am now in the best and final one.

Phase 1: Success

At 19 years old, I discovered the word "success". I wanted to be successful. My mistakes will hopefully save you YEARS of pursuing empty, dead-end goals.

The first mentor I ever had influenced me to believe that I could be and should be a millionaire by age 30. So, that's how I judged success.

Money and possessions were important at that time, but I believe I really just wanted other people to *view* me as successful. I didn't know what my definition of success was but looking back, I know I was more concerned about how *others* would view my success.

Phase 2: Significance

Around 22 years of age, I had some other mentors who conditioned me to shift from "success" to "significance". It felt right. It felt "others focused".

But over the course of about three years, I discovered that *aiming* to be significant is almost as selfish as aiming to be successful. In most cases, the motives of a person *aiming* to be significant are to have a bigger spotlight shone upon them. "Look at me, look at me!"

"I helped that person change their life," or, "Because of me, that athlete made it to college."

Significance was a really hard *intention* for me to shift away from. Significance can and should be the natural *result* of helping others, however it should not be your goal. It wasn't until I was about 25 that I learned a new way to define my life purpose from a mentor named Ken Blanchard.

Phase 3: Self-Surrendering Service

"Be especially careful when you are trying to be good so that you don't make a *performance* out of it. It might be good theater, *but the God who made you won't be applauding.*"

This comes from the book of Matthew in the Bible.

At age 25 I realized that I cared about God's opinion more than anyone else's. So, when I realized that He said *significance* was the wrong *aim*, I decided it was time to aim at a new target.

Rick Warren says it this way: "When you do something for someone else, don't call attention to yourself. When you help someone out, don't think about how it looks. Just do it – quietly and unobtrusively."

Was I doing what I was doing to give God glory or to enhance *my* story. Was it about *Him* or was it about *my legacy?*

Seriously, this was (and still is) *tough* for me to discern. I have to constantly check my motives. Legacy cannot be the goal. It's selfish when it's the primary ambition. *A great legacy is just an outcome of right living, just as winning a championship is an outcome of the coach and team focusing on the right stuff.*

Whether or not you are a believer, I am convinced that as a coach you must find a higher power to play for and coach for. Otherwise, the feedback loop on coaching youth is too long and oftentimes frustrating to the point of wanting to quit.

Those who coach for a higher power often find more purpose and meaning in their calling to coach. A higher power, like God, will help you to *power through* the unfruitful times, of which there will be many. There have been numerous times throughout my ten-year coaching career that I have asked, "Is it worth it? All the planning, program designing, dealing with difficult parents, dealing with the ungrateful and unmotivated athletes – I might give up and do something else that's *easier*, something that pays more."

And every time I ask that question, I am reassured by the Lord that it *is* worth it. It may be with a handwritten note from an athlete. It may be a text or email from a parent. It may be me closing my eyes and reflecting on the success story of a former athlete whom I helped. Remembering *why* you do what you do is important, but I have personally found that only comes when you have a *who* that you are doing it *for.*

Absent a higher power, you still must identify your guiding moral compass for decision making as a coach. You will still need to find a constant source of love and fuel that is poured into *you*, so that your emotional and spiritual bucket remains filled. You and I cannot pour from an empty bucket. We cannot give what we ourselves do not receive consistently. And since no human being can fulfill the love needs that you and I have, I concluded that choosing to receive *God's unfailing and unending love* was the best option.

Self-surrendering service is my new focus. It's my new *aim*. It means I lay down my own agenda, my own ambitions, and my own desires in order to help others realize that being a servant-leader who is others-centered is the best way to live life.

We, as coaches, need to constantly and relentlessly battle against the "what's in it for me" mentality. We must actively flee from self-promotion.

Babies and Dogs – the Greatest is the Servant

My pastor recently gave a hilarious but profound illustration. Imagine if aliens from outer space, foreign to the way humans "did life," were able to watch the interactions between parents and babies, as well as with owners and dogs.

I bet those aliens would say, "*Wow!* Look at that little creature [the baby]. That baby must be the most powerful creature in all the land! Look at the way the bigger creature [parent] serves the little one. It changes its diaper, it feeds the little one, it does *everything for the little one!*

And look at the furry creature [the dog]. It too must be powerful! Look how the bigger one goes around and cleans up its poop and brushes its hair! The furry one pulls the bigger one around by the rope!"

It all came full circle for me as my pastor gave this silly illustration. The reason the parent serves their baby is because the parent is *greater* than the baby. And the reason the owner serves the dog is because the owner is *greater* than the dog. The one who is greater is created to *serve* the one who is less – who knows less, has less, and is less.

Coaches, this is why *we* are wise to be servants to our student-athletes. We are greater – for now. Our job is to serve them, care for them, and help them grow so that they can go on to be greater and serve others one day as well.

When you let this truth sink in and you meditate over the implications of it in your coaching philosophies, it could literally change your entire organization as it has mine. For parents, it can absolutely do the same for your family, business, and even your social circles.

Servant leadership in action is so beautiful and contagious that those who experience it firsthand cannot help but to be transformed from the inside out.

Here is why I am so passionate about servant-leadership. Nothing I have is my own. I was served by mentors and coaches who came before me. I was redeemed and restored by my Father who decided to give me influence and power to inspire others. With great power comes great responsibility. And if I do inspire someone to change their life in a positive way, I cannot take the credit. I don't want it. Otherwise, I will fall back into the trap of seeking selfish significance, doing things for *others* to see. That, to me, is a sign of an insecure, sad, unfulfilled life. I do not want that to be the legacy that I leave behind.

This is *my* philosophy and *my* why. It may not be yours, *but you need to have one.*

You need to stand for something definitive as a coach or you will fall for anything. What are the core values and principles on which you will build your team, your family, and/or your organization? A house built on sand will fall when the storm comes, but, the house built on rock will not be shaken.

Are you ready to commit to a life of self-surrendering service? The state of our youth is not good. The youth sports industry as a whole is in bad shape. There is a movement happening that is going to transcend the current state of our student-athletes across the globe. Will you be a part of it?

Summary of Introduction

- Take a quick survey of your athletes. Are there any you are concerned about emotionally or mentally?

- Don't get so caught up in the outer shell of success that you can't see the inner struggles of your kids.

- The things that get the bulk of your time are your priorities. Audit your time quarterly.

- Imagine. What can you see? What is your vision for the future of youth athletics and the impact you'll make?

- Don't be silent. Speak out against the problems you see and be the solution.

- Everything rises and falls on leadership. You are the problem *and* the solution.

- What do you *believe* about your role? Your purpose? This determines everything else that follows, and ultimately, the results for your athletes.

- Who am I not being that my player's eyes are not shining? What do I need to personally change about myself, my attitude, my character?

- Writing creates clarity. If you want to see your athletes have breakthroughs mentally and emotionally, have them write.

- What are your three end-of-life questions? The questions determine your effectiveness today.

- Kids crave mindset coaching. They want to go deep, and they need your help.

- Self-surrendering service and sacrifice is the highest honor.

Part 1

SHINING A SPOTLIGHT ON THE CURRENT STATE OF OUR YOUTH

Chapter 1

ANXIETY IS AT AN ALL-TIME HIGH

According to the National Institute of Mental Health, an estimated 31.1% of U.S. adults experience an anxiety disorder at some time in their lives (https://www.nimh.nih.gov/health/statistics/any-anxiety-disorder.shtml).

Interestingly enough, an estimated 31.9% of *adolescents* had an anxiety disorder. And the number is *climbing* (https://www.nimh.nih.gov/health/statistics/any-anxiety-disorder.shtml).

We need to pay attention to these types of statistics. The fact that anxiety is *climbing* means what we are doing is not working. If you're like me, you take these statistics personally and have a burning desire inside to help as many as possible to overcome anxiety without the long-term use of medication.

Note: I understand there are cases where medication may be needed and/or beneficial. But I have personally seen mindset performance coaching help a kid overcome their anxiety. Training the mind, body, emotions, and spirit is stronger than any pill you'll ever find.

Another youth truth is that burnout from sports is also at an all time high. Which makes sense. You'd burnout too if you were anxious all the time.

According to multiple organizations, burnout is at an all-time high. The organization *Athlete Types* reports that an estimated 70% of athletes burn out and quit sports by the age of 13. The two reasons they state are coaches and parents. There is too much pressure and it is "just not fun anymore." Two additional reasons are that kids are sick of getting injured and sick of being belittled by coaches.

Statistics *are* important to look at. However, I see over 600 different student-athletes every year, and all I need to do is study their body language when they walk in our doors.

Try it one time. Ask your athletes: "On a scale of 1-10, 10 meaning you LOVE sports and are as passionate as ever about playing them, and 1 meaning that you are really not enjoying sports, where are you?"

In February 2019, I had the opportunity to meet Drew Brees, Super Bowl-winning quarterback of the New Orleans Saints, and ask him a question: "Drew, why is burnout at an all-time high and growing?"

His simple, powerful response: "Andrew, sports gets too serious too fast."

I personally know 10-year-olds who are on two club teams, have private hitting coaches year-round, and do sports performance training on top of it. They have no life. Parents can put a stop to it if they really wanted to, and they would want to if they took the time to really think about the long-term ramifications of that kind of life for a 10-year-old. Coaches can also put a stop to it.

My good friend Leslie Trujillo, Strength and Conditioning Coach, best-selling author of *Dear Her*, and founder of the Convos with Coaches podcast, says that the biggest problem in youth sports is the *business* it has become. How big is the youth sports business?

Sixty million participants and $15 billion annually.

Club coaches want athletes with them all year because it means more money for them. Trainers want athletes with them year-round because it means more money for them. Private skill coaches, same thing. The question we always ask ourselves as coaches at PFP is, "What is the best thing for the athlete at this point in time?" It is a question I do not believe many are asking, which is why burnout is at an all-time high. The more common question I believe is, "What's in it for me?"

If your athletes seem to be drained, you need to stop asking the question, "What do I need to *do* to motivate them?"

Instead of asking the *what* question, you should be asking, "*Why* are our athletes not fully energized and engaged in their sport anymore?"

Maybe the more difficult question is many coaches and parents need to ask is, "Why am *I* not fully engaged and energized in my job and in my life right now?"

The apple doesn't fall far from the tree. There is truth to that saying. Energy, enthusiasm, and joy are transferred from coach to athlete, parent to child, and teacher to student. The kids I work with who are passionate and engaged in what they do have parents, teachers, and coaches who are living a fully charged and engaged life.

It is something to consider as a youth influencer. "Who do I need to be in order to see my athletes rise up?"

There is a current belief floating around today that "more is better" and it is contributing to the injury epidemic we are seeing in youth athletes today. We are addicted to *more* and it is costing our athletes big time.

Chapter 2

INJURIES ARE AT AN ALL-TIME HIGH

High school athletes account for an estimated two million injuries, 500,000 doctor visits, and 30,000 hospitalizations each year. That number is climbing.

Here are some frightening and eye-opening stats for you:

- According to the Centers for Disease Control, more than half of all sports injuries in children are preventable.

- Although 62 percent of organized sports-related injuries occur during practice, one-third of parents and coaches do not have their children take the same safety precautions at practice that they would during a game.

- Twenty percent of children ages eight to 12 – and 45 percent of those ages 13 to 14 – will experience arm pain during a single youth baseball season.

- Injuries associated with participation in sports and recreational activities account for 21 percent of all traumatic brain injuries among children in the United States.

- Children ages five to 14 account for nearly 40 percent of all sports-related injuries treated in hospitals. On average, the rate and severity of injury increases with a child's age.

- Overuse injuries are responsible for nearly half of all sports injuries to middle and high school students.

Those are some of the statistics. Is there a problem here? Yep – but there are also solutions.

(https://www.stopsportsinjuries.org/STOP/Resources/Statistics/STOP/Resources/Statistics.aspx?hkey=24daffdf-5313-4970-a47d-ed621dfc7b9b)

Chapter 3

THE PARADOX OF YEAR-ROUND SPORTS

Success leaves clues. The average professional athlete or Olympian takes three months off every year to focus on recovering, rejuvenating, and re-energizing. The one thing they do have year round are the world's best recovery specialists, which allows them to go hard for nine months, give or take. How about your youth athletes? Is there a planned period of rest and recovery, or are they just doing what everyone else is doing?

What are the positives of playing year-round?

- Skill development may go up temporarily
- There are more opportunities to get seen by college scouts, if you don't get hurt

The negatives of playing year-round:

- Risk of injury goes up
- Strength, speed, and power go down
- Joy, excitement, and love for sport goes down
- Burnout, stress, and overwhelm goes up
- Pressure to perform goes up
- Fear of falling behind goes up

You will need to decide what *you* value most. I think every athlete deserves to be aware of and educated on the repercussions of year-round sports. If you have been ignoring this, it is time to stop the avoidance. Avoidance is a great short-term strategy to be comfortable, but a long-term plan to be miserable.

The youth truth is that their bodies are not built to handle the intense year-round running, conditioning, and cutting, the excessive swinging, throwing, and twisting motions, and repetitive stress to the same muscles, joints, and ligaments. We need to have a 12 month formula in order to ensure our athletes health.

Chapter 4

SOLUTIONS TO THE INJURY EPIDEMIC

Overuse injuries mean that you overuse certain muscles because you overdo certain movements. With that said, can it even be argued that those who play multiple sports are less likely to sustain overuse injuries? Can it just be accepted as common sense that if you stop overusing certain muscles and overdoing certain movements, you will give yourself a better chance at avoiding overuse injuries?

I will leave it up to you to decide what makes sense. But looking at the statistics, what we are currently doing is not working. And at this point, we know the definition of insanity – doing the same things over and over again and expecting a different result.

Destiny's Story

Destiny's shin splints started in 11th grade. She played lacrosse year-round. It progressively got worse, and by the time she got to a Division I college program, the shin splints had turned into Compartment Syndrome. The worst part about all of this was she *knew* something was terribly wrong because her feet were going numb, but people kept telling her, "Stretch."

Side note: stretching but refusing to *rest* is like ordering a Big Mac and fries at McDonald's and then uttering a request to the cashier such as, "And a water, please."

The stretching, like the water, is obviously good for you, but it will do very little to combat the damage done from the excessive running.

Destiny had to sit out most of her freshman year. How *deflating!* She had a D1 scholarship and she couldn't even play her first year. And because she had some not-so-helpful coaches, they wrote her off and sat her on the bench in the spring.

Fast forward to the summer before her sophomore year. She recently had to have two surgeries to just have a *chance*, but the issue is still there.

She is in the middle of making one of the hardest decisions she has had to make, which is to save her body for the next 65+ years by quitting the game she loves earlier than she should have to. And this is at least partially because of all the wear and tear on the same muscles, tendons, and tissues over the past 10+ years. The brutal fact we need to face is that her coaches and parents did not put their foot down. The influencers did not make a definitive decision *for* Destiny. I could have, and I should have.

If you want to make a difference, stop giving suggestions and start being more aggressive. We know the problem is overuse and overplaying, which comes from deeper psychological fears and desires to please others and be accepted. Call it out from a place of care and candor, and don't let another one of your athletes' bodies get destroyed unnecessarily.

How to combat the injury epidemic:

1. Coaches must be willing to restructure schedules.

In order to rise up and stand out, you must be ahead of the curve and be willing to try something different.

    a. Plan for intermittent periods of time off from intense running and practicing your particular sport.

    b. Do not allow practices to last more than 90 minutes.

John Wooden never ran practice longer than 90 minutes and won 11 national championships.

Attention spans are getting shorter by the day. The results from recent studies showed the average human attention span has fallen from 12 seconds in 2000, or around the time the mobile revolution began, to eight seconds in 2017.

Shorter practices with increased intensity and focus are 10 times more effective.

2. **Parents and athletes must address their fears of falling behind and missing out and must recognize that less is often MORE.**

3. **Coaches will need to allocate more time and resources toward developing solid recovery and regeneration-based solutions for their athletes.**

4. **Coaches and parents need to shift from a reactive mindset to a more proactive one.** Kids should not be in the athletic training room more than they are on the practice field. Physical therapy should not be their second home.

5. **Have a PLAN to stay healthy:**

    a. Ten minutes of true warm up before practice and games, and 10 minutes of focused, effective recovery post practice

    b. One day *minimum* dedicated to *active* recovery each week – stretching, foam rolling, breathing, massage, etc.

    c. One day dedicated to complete rest each week

d. One de-load week *minimum* every 12 weeks. Scale back all lifting, running, cutting, high impact. Take that week to do deeper in *another* area of performance, e.g. mental game, team unity and team building, etc.

e. Twelve weeks off from "game speed play" per year from that given sport. If you play lacrosse, you better be willing to take 12 weeks off of game play and full speed running/ cutting.

It is said that the pain of discipline is far more enjoyable than the pain of regret. Choose to take 12 weeks off per year or a forced 12 weeks off due to injury will inevitably choose you.

Your 13 and 14-year-olds are going to be crippled 40 year old parents in chronic pain who cannot play with their kids because they were brainwashed as teen athletes to believe that putting their fragile bodies through pain 365 days a year was worth it, and wouldn't cause any long term damage. At least we can claim our kids, our players, our team were the best during that one season in 2019…

That may sound extreme, but the amount of time spent in boots, braces, hospitals, and physical therapy clinics *is also* extreme. The amount of money spend on reactive care before our kids are even old enough to drive is crazy, if you ask me.

No more short-sighted thinking. It is silly, narrow-focused, and cruel. Kids do not understand the principle of the Compound Effect like we do. They have not lived long enough to experience what happens when you do the *wrong things to your body* day after day, week after week, month after month, and year after year until "one day, all of the sudden", something really bad happens.

Is it OK to quit?

Another current youth truth is that the number of athletes who have the desire to play in college and the number who are actually finishing 4 years of playing is decreasing. This is due to the pain and frequency of injury becoming too great, the increase in pressure, the expectations, and the limited rewards and positive reinforcement they are receiving from coaching. On the other hand, the college coaches who teach life lessons and help their players become better people will see higher retention rates with their athletes.

There are a lot of kids striving to play college sports not because they really want to, but rather because they feel like they have to in order to meet expectations and be accepted. Wouldn't you agree that not all kids are meant to go to college for engineering, nursing, or physical therapy? The same is true here. We would be wise to stop pushing college sports as the standard for all high school athletes that decide to play club sports.

Back in February of 2019 I gave a presentation titled, **"When to QUIT vs. When to RECOMMIT"**, which is a BONUS resources you will receive in the link given later on in the book. I needed to teach our college athletes how to discern between when it was time to hang up the cleats versus when it was time to recommit to their sport. At PFP, a lot of what we teach our athletes comes from observing their struggles, as well as listening to recurring challenges they are facing.

Our "formula" as coaches at PFP is:

1. OBSERVE
2. LISTEN
3. CREATE SOLUTIONS

I recorded this webinar in response to many college athletes and parents trying to figure out why they were feeling so stressed, disengaged, unenthused, and anxious about their sport. We discovered many of them should have left the *organized game* a long time ago. Not the sport as a whole, but the rigor and demand of the organized, collegiate sport. I'll unpack the shocking results of that webinar later on.

But the point of this chapter is this: stop going along with the crowds. If you follow them too long you'll get lost in them. You can't stand out if you are blending in with every other team. You can't expect extraordinary results with your son or daughter if you are being an ordinary parent. And you cannot expect to see your athletes stay healthy if they keep doing what every other athlete is doing. Be different and choose to embrace the 12-month healthy athlete formula. Whether you knew it or not, you signed up for this. The injury epidemic is part of your fight.

Chapter 5

OWNING YOUR FIGHT

For some people, it's animal cruelty. When they hear about a poor little puppy who was abused by his/her owner, it fires them up and makes them want to cry at the same time.

For others, it's seeing women whose voices are suppressed and not empowered by their husbands. Homeless children. Racial discrimination. Malpractice by physicians. Dirty cops who abuse their power and fail to serve and protect. There are an infinite number of causes on which to take a stand.

But then there are the ones we were *created to fight for*. I believe I have been called to speak truth, love, and life into one particular arena at this stage in my life. Since you are reading this book, maybe this is your fight, too. I believe as coaches we need to take this fight more seriously, bring new firearms, more ammo, and a lot of heart.

What am I willing to die for?

It took a while after that experience at the nine-year-olds' recreational soccer game for me to begin to understand the magnitude of what was going on. What is happening truly does break my heart. Abusive, negligent coaches and parents living vicariously through their children are two big problems.

I find it troubling that many kids are no longer playing sports for enjoyment, but instead to impress people and maintain their status. They are playing and striving for greatness to please and impress their parents, coaches, and teammates. Just last summer I personally spoke with four collegiate athletes who admitted that they were only staying on the team because they didn't want to lose their friends and become lonely at college.

The *outcome* has superseded the *journey.*

Another youth truth based on our actions is that the idea of *"honoring the process"* really doesn't mean much anymore. The idea of **growing, trying, failing, learning, and becoming** the best you can be based on what you have been given is no longer the most important thing. What is clearly more important than the process is *the outcome.*

How do I know this? It is obvious and self-evident. What gets recognized and rewarded determines what is most important.

We need to recognize our own flaws. If you and I are honest, we can barely stand to see our kids fail. Many of us fear failure ourselves.

But if we fear failure to the point or paralysis in our own lives, our kids will never be able to rise up above *their* fears. This is the Law of the Lid. The people you lead will never exceed your level of growth in a given area, which in this case, is fear.

My suggestion is that you start with yourself. Then, start rewarding and recognizing your kids for trying even when they fail. Honor them for attempting something on the field that they were not quite ready for, even if it cost the team the game. Please, stop celebrating the kid who scored three goals *again* mainly because he went through puberty two years before everyone else.

Have a long-term vision for your athletes and your team. Show them by what you recognize and reward that you really do value the *process* over the *outcome*.

Chapter 6

WHERE HAS OUR CURRENT PARADIGM GOTTEN US?

A paradigm is the way we think about and view something. Your paradigms are usually based on *your* experience, research, current societal norms, theories, and what you have heard from other people.

I've concluded that confidence and self-belief take the biggest hit as a result of the current paradigm of sports. We've surveyed thousands of youth athletes and 99.8% say their confidence is like a roller coaster and they are not sure how to fix it. Most kids cannot even define what confidence is, they just know they don't have it and they want more of it.

Isn't it true that solving the problems of confidence and self-belief is different and more challenging than getting an athlete to run faster, jump higher, throw harder, or swim faster?

The encouraging thing is that there is no predetermined age that a person is allowed to become a confident, courageous leader. You do not have to wait until college to do this. Under your leadership, your athletes can learn things about life that many never learn.

It was Les Brown who once said, "I never let my schooling get in the way of my education." I think that is profound based on the fact that we have a school system that spends the bulk of its time teaching kids lessons that do not translate very well to life after school.

At age nineteen I began my *intentional growth journey.* The mentors I had, the books I read, and the exercises I completed allowed me to begin transforming my mind and consequently, my actions and results that followed. I took those same lessons and have been able to teach them to thousands of students ranging from seven all the way up to twenty-two years old. And because they are adaptable and work so well, I decided to make them part of our staff development to help our team members grow personally and professionally.

Just so you understand the results of delivering this new type of coaching to your athletes, I want you to know that we have helped 14-year-olds improve their time management. We have helped 11-year-olds avoid the comparison trap *before* ever falling into it. We have adapted that same lesson to 22-year-olds to help them *escape* the comparison trap before leaving college and entering into the real-world.

We have taught 10-year-olds about the people pleaser syndrome and the perfectionist mentality. And we've helped 19-year-olds *overcome* the fear of disappointing their parents, their coaches, and their teammates.

If you want to help your kids smash through their fears rather than avoiding them, stand for what they believe in, and guide them onto a path to becoming the person they were created to be, I recommend the following:

- Have more intense 1:1 conversations. We call these "Magic Moments".

- Build trust and respect and then give your kids personal growth books to read, videos to watch, and content to consume that is engaging and relevant.

- Create visual frameworks that help kids to understand life principles (or steal the ones in this book).

- Invest more time and money in your own personal development. You can *always* level this up. Learn how to be a better storyteller, or a better teacher by using analogies and metaphors to persuade.

- Do webinars for your athletes, send them personalized videos, and do live, in-person, workshops and seminars.

All you need to do to have a deeper, more transformative impact is to get outside of your traditional teaching or coaching box and shift your focus. It may sound exhausting on top of your already crammed schedule, but doing a little each day compounded over time is manageable.

If you are a parent, I hope you recognize that mentors can save your child years of unnecessary pain and heartache. The right mentors can help your kid to become more confident and successful far earlier than they would have otherwise. Three out of five young men and women grow up without a mentor. I want to see that number get to five out of five. If your child does not have one right now, start seeking with all your heart and soul and ask God to send one your way.

Chapter 7

THE PROBLEMS DEFINED

Below are some quick descriptions of how these problems kids are facing show up in their day-to-day actions and decisions. I believe these definitions are helpful before we get to the practical application.

#1 The Perfectionist Mentality

"That wasn't good enough."

"I should have done that better."

"If it isn't done perfectly it isn't worth doing."

All of these *learned perfectionist mindsets* can be shifted and used for the success and increased performance for your student-athlete. Perfect actually means, "to perfect".

#2 Conformity

Most kids today are so unsure of themselves and lacking clarity on who they are that they spend every day of their lives trying to be someone they are not. Someone once said to me, "Andrew, isn't it weird that people need help figuring out who they are nowadays? Like, it's *who they are*. Why do they need someone else to help them with that?"

"This is an interesting perspective," I thought. But my answer is this: There is more noise than ever before. Social media alone has made it necessary for all of us to do *daily soul searching*. We all need some initial guidance from a coach, mentor, or teacher to figure out who we really are, and than daily practice and accountability to remind ourselves so you don't fall into the comparison trap." People a hundred years ago would think this is a little odd, but it *is* necessary today. Once you know your values and become rooted in them, it becomes easier to be who you are and live it out boldly with conviction every day. We will get into this more in Part 4.

#3 Fear

This includes the fear of missing out, the fear of falling behind, the fear of failing, and the fear of making a mistake. It includes the fear of disappointing mom, dad, coaches, and teammates, the fear of not living up to the expectations set for them, and the fear of living in a brother or sister's shadow. Not to mention, the self-doubt and self-consciousness that arise from those fears.

This is what kids are battling in their minds every single day. None of us will ever be fearless. All of us can learn to fear less. And all of us can learn how to punch fear in the face everyday with courage.

Have you ever thought about the fact that fear comes from our ability to imagine a future that has not yet come? It is actually a gift. Being able to close your eyes and imagine *amazing* things is something we would never want to give up. Fear is just imagining not so-good outcomes. Teach your athletes not to fear fear. None of us want to give up our imaginations, therefore we just need to learn how to manage those fears, and then teach it to our kids.

#4 The Comparison Trap

This one is so pervasive in today's youth that it needs very little explanation. There are four things about the comparison trap every kid needs to know and understand.

1. You cannot compare yourself to another until you have *paused* long enough to consider what that person has had to give up in order to be who they are or get what they have.

2. Once you have done so, you have to decide if you are *willing* and even *able* to sacrifice what they have sacrificed. If you have not done this, you cannot compare.

3. You must understand that you will not be happier if you get what that person has. It will cause a temporary boost in self-esteem, but it will not last. Most kids understand the idea of the "moving target of happiness."

4. Never compare the beginning of your journey to the middle of someone else's.

#5 Being a Follower

There is an abundance of followers today but a shortage of leaders. Too many are just following others instead of living their own lives. If you, the influencer, are not *inspiring, motivating, and teaching them* how to be a leader, who is? Leadership, when taught well, should inspire someone to want to lead. It is challenging, noble, and rewarding. Who *wouldn't* want that?

#6 People Pleaser Syndrome

Many kids have come to believe that the only way mom, dad, or coach will be proud of them is if they get first place, score points, earn first team all-conference, get on the honor roll, or get the scholarship. The result is that the fear of failing and disappointing causes stress, anxiety, and obviously the decreased performance that comes with those things.

#7 Immaturity: Low Mental and Emotional Resiliency

An inability to handle life's curveballs with poise and confidence. An inability to stay positive and optimistic despite a coach, teacher, or friend cutting you down with insults. I believe part of my mission as a love-powered leader is to help kids get better here.

I define immaturity as the following: *Immaturity is allowing your circumstances, the opinions of, and the actions of other people to dictate YOUR responses along with the way you think and feel about yourself.*

We came up with this definition during the summer of 2019 when our college athletes came home to train with us. About 20 male and females who had just finished up their freshman year were shaken.

"Coach was awful. I got injured and sat out during fall ball. This led to teammates gossiping about me. Coaches told me to reconsider college sports. I couldn't score like I used to in high school. I fell behind in school. I'm worthless, not cut out for this."

"No, you are immature and we need to build you up to be more mature this summer. Your past experiences make you stronger, they do not inherently have the power to determine the way you feel about yourself, your belief in yourself, or what is possible for your future - that is, unless you *let them.*"

Unshakeable confidence is what we needed to help our youth develop. Why?

Because our youth today have a low understanding of what it truly means to *be proactive*. Being proactive means having the ability to choose the way you will *respond* - to anything, to anyone, to any circumstances.

Response-ability.

I think adults struggle with this as much as kids, but when you learn this principle as a teenager or younger, it can make a profound difference in the way you think, act, and live your life. The weather does not have the power to influence your mood. Your coach's opinion of you, your performance, your work ethic, or your future abilities does not have to become your reality.

No person or thing has the inherent power to affect your mood, confidence, feelings, or actions.

It is our choice to give another person that power. You will be relieved when you get to the exercises in Part 4. They will help your athletes overcome all of the problems listed above.

What is "Normal"?

"Teenagers just are the way they are." I hate that. Is it really *normal* for a teenager to compare herself to everyone else, to act out to get attention, and to have anxiety before sporting events?

"She's a 14-year-old girl, that's why she's doing that! It's just normal teenager stuff."

It might be *the norm*, but it is not normal. And I don't know about you, but I don't want a normal kid. No thank you. I'll take different and unique and chalk that up as a *leader* any day of the week.

We get what we expect.

If we expect our kids to be immature, anxious, unable to deal with conflict, bad communicators, depressed, stressed, burnt out, injured, followers, or cowards (harsh words, but it's the current truth for most teenagers)...if we expect those things, than that is exactly what we will get.

Can you raise your expectations without putting unrealistic pressure on your kids? Is it possible to balance *believing* your kids can be different but not *demanding* it or condemning and criticizing them when they fail? It all lies in the art of casting a vision for someone that they cannot see themselves. It is the art of encouraging and building up another person. It is not easy, but you can do it.

Equipped with the love-powered leadership tools you can help your student-athletes to experience confidence, self-belief, and true foundational success *long before* most other kids do.

Chapter 8

DON'T GIVE YOUR ATHLETES THE WRONG MEDICINE

"As any doctor can tell you, the most crucial step toward healing is having the right diagnosis. If the disease is precisely identified, a good resolution is far more likely. Conversely, a bad diagnosis usually means a bad outcome, no matter how skilled the physician."
-- ANDREW WEIL

Imagine this: you are having severe stomach pains and constipation, so you get a CT scan ordered for your chest and abdomen. You are referred to a gastroenterologist. When you get there, the gastro starts talking with you about the findings of the CT scan immediately.

"John, everything with your stomach looks good. Based on your symptoms, I am going to prescribe you a stool softener to get things moving."

You get the stool softener, it works, and your stomach pain is gone.

Six months later you begin to have trouble breathing – severe trouble. A month goes by, and now you have excruciating neck and shoulder pain to go along with it. What is going on?

You have another CT scan ordered along with an MRI, and you go see a pulmonologist to discuss the results. The pulmonologist breaks the news to you that you have a huge mass on your left lung. It's cancer, and it has started to spread. You are crushed. You remember back to the first CT scan six months prior with the gastro.

"How did the gastro not see it six months ago? With the size of the mass now, it had to have been there," you think to yourself.

What happens next is the scariest reality that we all have to face, even as coaches.

You call the gastro up that day. "Doc, I was just diagnosed with stage three lung cancer. It's bad. Were there any signs of this six months ago when we met?"

"Yes, of course," he replies.

"You had a mass on your left lung when I reviewed your scan. However, you came to me for stomach problems, and I am, after all, a stomach doctor. Did the stool softeners help?"

Poor Diagnostics, Poor Prescriptions

Do not be this doctor for your athletes - the doctor that is too busy with a thousand other "patients" that you cannot go deep enough to provide an accurate diagnosis.

Do not be the doctor that corrects the *easiest, most profitable problems*. Choose the hard, less traveled path. The problems we talked about before *are* more damaging than their bad running form or poor stamina (both of which need to be fixed as well).

A turning point for you right now could be to make the decision to help your kids with the things that will change their life, not just their bat swing.

Chapter 9

SHADOWS WITHOUT SUBSTANCE

In 2015 I realized a major flaw in our approach to developing athletes. I surveyed all of our sports parents and asked them the question all coaches should ask more often:

"What area do you want to see your son or daughter *improve* in most? What do they struggle with *most*?" These two questions address the only two human narratives, *Struggle and Progress*. At any given moment we are all trying to either overcome struggle, or make progress. The thing about struggle is that it typically needs to be addressed *before* progress can be made

The parents responses, in order of most importance, were as follows:

1. Improve confidence

2. Belief in himself, or herself

3. To stop being a follower and become a leader

4. To be happy and have more joy

5. Make better decisions and avoid going down a bad path

6. Attitude: learn how to better manage their frustrations and emotions on and off the field

7. To be healthy physically, mentally, emotionally, and spiritually

8. To achieve their dreams and earn a scholarship

What is sad is that many parents *say* those things above matter, but then their actions revealing otherwise.

Example

Parent: "Greg is struggling, Andrew. He has low confidence and low self-esteem. He compares himself to others way too often. I'll do anything to help him overcome this."

Me: "Well, we have an 'Escape the Comparison Trap and Build Confidence' workshop this weekend. Want to sign Greg up?"

Parent: "I'll have to get back to you, we might get him a couple extra sessions this week with his hitting coach before tryouts next week."

Strength, speed, stamina, skill, and overall athleticism enhancement will never solve the deep-rooted struggles and desires that Greg has.

It seems like a little thing, but his mom's decision to prioritize physical training over the possibility of him having a life-changing breakthrough is a big, big problem. There are no inconsequential moments in life. Everything matters. Every decision has a cost.

As we will reinforce over and over again throughout this book, *coaches* have the most influence in a kid's life over any other youth influencer, which means *we* have the power to help with all of those deep desires. But it all starts with a different kind of coaching. It must come from a different place.

Chapter 10

A NEW APPROACH

After observing many coaches around the country I began to recognize that many said they trained the body, the heart, *and* the minds of their athletes, but it wasn't true.

Wouldn't you agree that the *proof* of a job well done as a coach shows up when a kid is *tested*? Would you agree that great coaching could be defined by seeing a positive, progressive change in your athletes' self-beliefs, attitudes, behaviors, actions, and results? If a kid gets faster and stronger but has not made any progress in his or her ability to keep a positive attitude in the face of adversity, are they improving their mental resiliency?

Best-selling author Timothy Jennings says that the *heart* is where our core identity lies. It is where our deepest desires, our most secret self, our deep-rooted beliefs about ourselves, and our character lie. Therefore, if we want to really help a young man or woman improve the trajectory of their lives and positively impact their futures, we must go to work on *the heart*.

The body and the mind are insufficient training grounds for lasting change.

This is why traditional sports psychology alone does not transform a kid's life. It may help their mind, but that is only one piece of the pie.

If the athletes you work with have not developed a new *belief* about fear, failure, and mistakes, will they ever *be* a "go for it" person who takes risks in life? Probably not. Because if they *believe* failure and mistakes are bad, they will *ultimately avoid those things*. Techniques and tactics to overcome fear will be short-lived if the beliefs in their *heart* have not changed.

For me, this new coaching pursuit was about helping teens make wiser decisions and develop a more confident, resilient mindset *as early in life as possible*. We saw an opportunity to teach what was not being taught ubiquitously in the sports and school systems. As an athletic performance coach, I decided to face the brutal facts of reality.

Playing sports, getting faster and stronger, doing homework, and studying was not *directly* helping any kids to improve many of those things I listed above.

If we want to make the deepest impact possible, there is no other choice as coaches but to go to work on the *hearts* of our athletes. Part 2 of this book will do a deeper dive into *how* to train the heart, but you as a coach must *believe* this work matters.

The experiences with my dad and my sisters that I mentioned in the introduction inspire me to want to be a more *love-powered coach*.

In the case of my sisters, I could only imagine how it would have ended if my parents and I led with authority, logic, facts, and figures about the effects of drug use instead of leading with love.

What changes people, really?

Love does. Unconditional love transforms people because of how uncommonly beautiful it is.

Love means going against our *logic and feelings*, and instead, choosing to love our kids where they are.

You must *love your athletes where they are if you want them to get to where you believe they can go.*

Love wins every time. But you cannot give what you have not received. Have you *received* love in abundance yet? If not, there is a constant source you can tap into right now that is so full, amazing, and consistent that it will fill your love bucket when no one else can.

Prepare to take your influence and impact to another level. To do so, you will need the ultimate tool that is proven to transform people from the inside out. It is the tool in your toolbox that may need "de-rustifying." It may need to be used a few times before you see real, lasting change. However, when you use this tool, when you apply this set of timeless principles I am about to share with you, the result is a *peak* performing student-athlete on the field as well as off the field. It is called Love-Powered Leadership.

Summary of Part 1:
The Problems Defined

- Anxiety is at an all-time high. Coaches can make a difference.

- Injuries are at all-time highs. Consider the long-term repercussions and make bold, uncommon changes to the way you plan your year, your season, and your weeks.

- While skills may increase with year-round sports, the downside outweighs the upside.

- Attention spans are too low to run productive practices longer than two hours. Lower the duration, increase the intensity, sit back, and watch the magic happen at game time.

- The fear of missing out and falling behind must be overcome daily.

- The pain of discipline is better than the pain of regret. Choose to take time off or be forced to.

- When it comes to your athletes' main struggles, the formula is: observe, listen, create solutions.

- Immaturity is allowing your circumstances and the opinions of others dictate your mood and actions. This is your baseline to determine whether or not you are helping your athletes mature.

- Just because it's the norm doesn't mean it's normal. Choose to be an uncommon coach and watch how you achieve uncommon results.

- Sports used to help kids build character. But because of the societal shift to elitism and our values getting more out of whack, sports are now doing more harm than good.

Part 2

LOVE-POWERED LEADERSHIP PRINCIPLES

Chapter 11

WHAT DOES LOVE REQUIRE OF ME?

"The opposite of love is not hate, but fear."
-- Jack Alexander, The God Guarantee

In his book *The God Guarantee*, Jack Alexander says that the opposite of love is not hate, but rather *fear*. After reflecting on what this means from a coach's perspective, it became a major a-ha moment for me.

Our business is year-round. However, like most businesses, there are certain seasons where it really booms, and others where is tapers off. Earlier in my career, I would start to anticipate the "down times" and then begin preparing to do whatever it took to keep athletes coming in our doors twice a week during their seasons. I would craft motivational emails, sales letters, videos, and everything else I could think of to keep all these kids coming in our doors. I did so partially because I thought it would be best for them to stay, but partially because I did not want our team and organization to lose a bunch of money! I certainly did not ask the one question that every selfless, love-powered coach should ask: "What does love require of me in this situation?"

You know what took over my mind?

FEAR.

"What if we do not have enough money to pay the bills?" Selfish.

"What if others notice that people are leaving, and they leave too?" Selfish.

"What if our coaches stop making money and THEY leave to go to a new gym?" Selfish.

The common denominator among all those questions is *me* – US. It was not focused on the kid. I've since learned that doing the right thing is always the best thing.

Fear, on the other hand, is the opposite of love, and it caused me to become self-centered rather than others focused. This kind of thinking has infected club sports coaches, personal trainers, college recruiters, and anyone who is trying to capitalize on the multi-billion-dollar industry of youth athletics.

If you fear losing your job because your team is not winning, you may revert to various manipulative forms of "motivation" and punishment for your players. If you have a deep-rooted fear of what others think about you, it will show up in your coaching. If you value achievement above all else, then the *fear* what other coaches or parents think of your coaching if your team underperforms will drive unloving forms of leadership. You will probably only play your starters and never give a kid who *could* be great a chance. This is unwise for coaches, because inevitably, at some point, the starters will get hurt or tired and the non-starters will have to play.

Do you have a fear that you will not measure up to the expectations others have placed on you as a coach? Be careful not to make your next move from this place of fear.

Giving in to fear always results in short-term thinking and decision making. It causes you and me to operate with a microwave mentality. But the greatest coaches think like chess players – two, three, ten moves ahead. They plant seeds for the future and avoid satisfying temporary needs. This is how the New England Patriots became a dynasty. Coach Bill Belichick did not let fear dictate his strategy.

Coach, have you ever let your fears keep you from loving your players well? What about your coaching staff? If you've been a coach for longer than a day, I can almost guarantee your answer is *yes*.

What does love require of me in this situation? How would love show for this player? For my kid? These are great foundational questions to ask yourself when you feel *fear* rising up inside.

This section of the book is all about love. Personally, I've found in my leadership that love is the solution. And when you see what love actually is in regard to leadership and coaching, I think you will agree it is more than just a feeling. It is transformational. It is the solution to 99% of your problems with your players, your team, your organization, and even your family.

Love is so critical to understand on a *functional level* that John Wooden, whom I will refer to often throughout the book, said that one of the greatest mistakes he made in his lifetime was leaving the word "love" out of his book, ***The Pyramid of Success.*** He said if he could go back and do it all over, he would have stuck the word "love" smack dab in the middle of that pyramid.

Wooden is arguably the greatest college basketball coach of all time. I do not need to know him personally to heed his counsel. He speaks, I listen. His results and track record with his players precede him.

Let's dive into what it would mean to make a love shift in your coaching style. For some of us it may be a minor shift, while for others it might be major. Regardless, we all need to make shifts if we want to keep growing and serving at a higher level.

Chapter 12

THE COACHING SHIFT

"Who your kids become in this life is more important than what they accomplish."

-- UNKNOWN

During my quiet time on the morning of March 10, 2019, I had another pretty big "a-ha moment." I knew I had changed as a coach. I knew I was way better at motivating, connecting with, getting through to, inspiring, and helping our athletes get better results. But I was not totally sure *why* until that morning.

I realized that over the last four years of my coaching career, something had changed. When you are in the weeds all day long, it is hard to get above it all and draw conclusions about what is really working and why.

Our business quadrupled in size during those four years. We doubled the size of our team. We were able to keep kids in our doors year-round when no other business in our industry was successfully doing so. We started seeing 75-100 kids come through our doors for small group training in just one evening.

"How did we keep athletes in our doors year-round when kids are busier than most CEOs nowadays!?

The *coaching shift* that we made increased retention, but more importantly, it increased the *impact* we were making in their lives. More confident, courageous servant-leaders were actually being developed inside those four walls. Remember, people don't do things for very long that they don't *want* to do and do not *need* to do. You have to create an environment that people want *and* need in order for them to keep coming back.

Over the course of these four years, what blew me away and humbled me were the testimonies of kids and parents who wrote to us saying things like:

"Thank goodness you are in my child's life. The mentoring he received from your team has changed him."

"I would bring my kid to you even if she never picked up a weight. It is the *way* you coach her... she does not get this anywhere else."

"He is a different person when he comes to you guys. You are like his church for the week."

"Jessi builds her schedule around coming to the gym now, even though she never used to plan anything. She shares more of her life with *me* now. She feels more confident because of the messages you share with the kids before the workouts."

"John responds to getting knocked down better now. He is actually staying positive and optimistic. What a difference."

"My relationship with my Addy is whole again."

"Ashley finally mustered up the courage to leave her old group of friends who were going down a bad path. It was that one motivational message you gave her last week about being the average of the five people you hang with the most."

"Alex's anxiety is gone. She is no longer taking medication."

These are real stories that happened when this one particular coaching shift was made. It is so simple that even a caveman could do it. But it is not easy. The coaching shift that changed everything for us is that we decided *love* would be the operating principle on which our culture of coaching was built. Our coaching methods and decisions would filter through this principle of love. For us, love means coaching our kids in a way that impacts them at the *heart level.*

Jeff Duke, creator of the powerful 3Dimensional Coaching program, says, "If you want to maximize performance and potential, today's players must be driven by their heart."

Craig Groeschel, leader of Life Church and the creator of the YouVersion Bible App, said it this way: *"The quickest way to change someone's mind is to connect with their heart."*

My goal is to get the kids I work with to do what I think they should do. I try to get them to do what *I think* will benefit *them* the most. The mistake I made for years is that I tried to change their *minds* before changing their *hearts*. Once you better understand the heart and how it functions on an emotional level, you will become a coach of greater influence.

Chapter 13

GOING DEEP TO IGNITE CHANGE

Your heart is what's on the *inside.* It is what holds your *core identity* and your *beliefs* about who you are and if you really matter or not.

It is your *innermost, secret self.*

It is your *character.*

It is where your *fears, doubts, and deepest longings and desires reside.*

If you cannot penetrate the heart, you cannot win someone over, inspire them to believe they are a leader, motivate them to reach their full potential, help them stop making poor decisions, or coach them in any other way that results in *lasting change.*

So how do you coach the heart? In Parts 3 and 4, we give you practical ways to do so at practice or at home. These are the actual lessons and exercises that we use to impact our athletes every day.

Michael's Story

In 2017, we started working with a teenage student-athlete named Michael. He was the epitome of an Eeyore. He was negative or emotionless. But day after day, week after week, we strived to give him love. Our team greeted him with a loving smile, hug, and a genuine "how are you?" As I worked with him in the gym, I helped him clean his weights up, I served him as best I could. I told him "I am proud of you" as often as I could. I challenged him to do more. I got together with him outside of the gym. Over time I began asking him questions like, "What are you afraid of?" I would always follow up with a text that day so that he would know "Coach is thinking about me."

"The fortune is in the follow up," my mentor once told me. The ultimate "fortune" for me in this case was a relationship where Michael would trust me and value my opinion enough to listen and take action. That was my end goal.

During my first five years of coaching athletes, I did not think like this. I did not know how to begin with the end in mind. I did not have end objectives. I just showed up with my stopwatch each day and my "plan" was to help athletes get better. Motivated but ignorant, I failed to make the impact that I was capable of making.

I studied Michael's parents during this time as well. I noticed his dad was Negative Norman – bad attitude. It was likely that he was the type of guy that came home after a long, stressful day and was rude, stand-offish, and short-tempered with his wife and kids. But I wasn't positive about that, so I had to do some digging. I wanted to see if Michael would share with me a little about his dad.

My assumption was accurate. I asked Michael point blank, "I see that your dad's negative attitude has rubbed off on you over the years. How would you like to move forward? How do you want your younger brothers and sisters to be?"

"How" is the best word to start a question. I learned this from a former Head of Negotiations at the FBI, Chris Voss. "How" gets the

person thinking deeper. "Why," on the other hand, puts people on the defensive. Rather than opening up, they will close themselves off.

Michael was given the beautiful opportunity of *choice* that day. He got to choose the type of person he wanted to be. Through journaling, reflection, and then discussion with me, he had breakthroughs.

The kids you work with do not have to become anything they do not want to be. Neither do you. We all have the power to choose our destiny. And I believe that it is *our* job as coaches to help them help themselves. It is in our power to open up doors of possibility for these kids to walk through.

Kind, loving, resilient, positive, optimistic, pleasant, present, engaged, enthusiastic – these are traits of the most joy-filled, successful people in the world. They are traits that are universally good. They are undeniably attractive.

Don't get me wrong: no two people are alike, and no one should be put into a box they do not want to be in. But at the end of the day, this is the character foundation we need to strive to build in every single kid we work with!

I know I have to *display* what these things look like through my words, actions, and reactions. I want to inspire my athletes to create positive change in their lives and then give them the power and tools needed so that they can choose who they want to be.

Today, Michael is playing soccer at a higher level. But more importantly, he and his mom have good conversations. I see him smiling with her before and after sessions. He opens up and engages with his siblings, something that would have *never* happened if we did not begin with the end in mind. We have helped him create *reasons why* he wants to be a more positive, happy person. And those reasons go far beyond him helping himself.

Love wins, coach. It always wins. Here is what it looks like in action.

Chapter 15

LOVE-POWERED COACHING

HEART-WRENCHING.

When I watch kids *fight for something that should be freely given,* it is like a knife to my gut.

How many kids do you know who try to run faster, jump higher, beat the other kid, win the medal, and get stronger in an attempt to be seen, for others to notice them? The truth about the youth today is that most do this because they are craving two things. And these are two things that you crave, that I crave, and that they will crave for the rest of their lives:

Love and acceptance.

Steph's Story

Steph walked in our doors in September 2017. I noticed pain in her eyes right away. She had numerous medical conditions that made it all but impossible for her to play sports. She was overweight and struggling to find a friend group who accepted her.

We have a questionnaire that every student fills out when they start training at PFP. They highlight the statements that are true for them. For example:

My parents put a lot of pressure on me to play well.

If it is at all true, we ask them to highlight it. We let the athlete fill it out on their own, then we come back and discuss their answers. It is truly astonishing how honest kids are when they are asked to *self-identify by circling or highlighting answers* opposed to having to verbalize them. There is a great system to this that I will share with you later in the book.

I said to Steph, "You know the reason why this one is on the list?"

"Why?" she asked.

"Because you are not the only one. Hundreds of kids just like you are struggling with this, too. Can you tell me more about your parents putting pressure on you to play well?"

I was not expecting the response I got next.

"Last weekend, my dad locked me in my room with no water, food, or cell phone for six hours because I struck out twice."

(Side note: she is OK, so you can laugh at the fact that she put her cell phone right up there with the survival necessities of food and water.)

She went on to tell me that this is a regular punishment for poor performance. Whether or not this was 100% true or not is irrelevant. Because if she was lying, there was an even more frightening reason *why*. To make something up like that to get attention would reveal an even deeper issue. But I know that this was at least partially true because there are literally hundreds of variations of this same story I have heard over the past 10 years.

I don't know about you, but the two people I wanted unconditional love from the *most* in my life were my mom and dad. Whether I failed, struck out, or stole a pack of baseball cards from a store, I still needed them to love me. And they did.

As coaches, it is our job to bridge the gap. We must stand boldly in the discomfort and let the parents know what is *really* going on. Becoming a legacy coach requires engaging in difficult conversations whenever you are called to. And if you are a parent, I know you love your kids. I hope the stories in this book will help you to see opportunities to bring more unconditional, love-powered *parenting* to the sports side of your family life.

I talked with both parents about their daughter's accusation. It was not fun, but the result was *change*. Their relationship is getting better every day.

What does love NOT look like?

I *love* this quote by an unknown author that says, "Love is not 'if' or 'because.' Love is 'anyway,' 'even though,' and 'in spite of.'"

These kids want *so badly* to be better *loved* and *accepted* by their parents, coaches, teammates, peers, and now by their social media followers, that they will do anything to get it.

Consider for a moment what the *opposite* of love would look like in *your role* in the development of a youth athlete. The opposite of love is:

- **The pre-game reminders** that scream, "To make me proud, you better do well as defined by the scoreboard, stat book, and what others consider success." (Conditional love)

- **The dissatisfaction in our voices** when our athlete underperforms. (Conditional love)

- **Our body language** when our athlete fails to beat the other. (Conditional love)

- **Our inconsistency in our response** to good games and bad games. (Conditional love)

- **Our lack of recognition** for things like effort, selflessness, or for them staying positive even though they made an error. Instead, we put our athletes in the spotlight only when they achieve great stats. (Conditional love)

If your athlete is constantly striving to be the *best* or to *impress*, I recommend doing some digging. Try to find out if it is from the natural drive in their heart and their love for the game *or* if it is an **outward expression of an inward cry** for your unconditional love and acceptance.

The Say NOTHING Challenge

My team and I created a challenge back in June 2019 called "The Say NOTHING Challenge." I will refer to this challenge throughout the book. It was ultimately a way for sports parents to get better at using athletic competitions as a vehicle to *display* unconditional love to their athletes. The results were phenomenal. One parent in particular literally experienced *life-altering results* for her daughters.

"As a parent of young athletes, I found myself getting increasingly impatient with them and their performance. I couldn't discern WHY I was getting like this. Was it my personal drive for excellence that I was putting on them? What if they weren't 'created' to be amazing athletes? Was I unknowingly comparing them and their performance to the other kids on the team, and therefore getting embarrassed when my kids weren't the best? What was I turning into? I had forgotten that this was a GAME. Taking part in this challenge didn't make me a better sports parent, it made me a better leader for my family, for my kids. Love IS the answer. Sometimes it requires discipline. Sometimes

it requires me to be quiet. I want to love my kids because of who they are, not what they do or do not accomplish in a game." -Kerry

Whether you are a coach or parent, the implications of this are far reaching. In Part 4 of the book, I have a practical experiment for *coaches* to try that will be tough and counter-intuitive, but I can all but guarantee it will result in a poised, confident athlete.

When fear, doubt, and worry are removed, all that remains is a joy-filled, passionate athlete primed and ready for success.

Love-Powered Coaching

I've used one primary source to transform the way I coach today's generation of youth athletes, as well as the way I coach our team of coaches. The Bible is packed with motivation and inspiration for coaches to lead better.

Before we go there, it is important to remember that love is *universal,* it is *functional,* and it is *practical.* It is *not* a feeling. The principle of love and the concept of heart-centered coaching has the power to positively impact anyone's life, especially the lives of kids who seldom receive real love from youth influencers. Most would not argue against the fact that unconditional love in action makes everything and everyone better.

If you are a coach or parent who has ever struggled to motivate or *influence* your athletes in any way, this is the one ingredient you need to double or triple up on in your coaching recipe.

The transformational impact of love should not be a surprise, since *giving* love is hard, especially when it is hard. We all know that the most beneficial time to do something is when it is hard and when we do not feel like it. As the saying goes, "Successful people do the things consistently that unsuccessful people do occasionally."

When an athlete disobeys you, fails, and messes up over and over again even after you have taught them well, *this* is when love is hardest to give but needed the *most*. Love is supremely influential when given at the *right time*. It transforms athletes on that *heart level that we discussed earlier.* We all love hearing stories of leaders who did the right thing despite it being difficult to do. You never feel like giving love at those critical times, but you and I would both be wise to work on it.

There is an overplayed verse in the Bible that teaches *how* love acts. You hear it at every wedding, but rarely in terms of leading or coaching. This type of love was demonstrated perfectly through the life of Jesus.

Most people nowadays, Christian or not, acknowledge that Jesus *was* a living, breathing person, and his acts of *love* are strongly documented and corroborated by historical evidence. Even if you do not share my beliefs, I know you will find this section on *love* both practical and transformational as a love-powered coach.

*"**4** Love is patient, love is kind. It does not envy, it does not boast, it is not proud. **5** It does not dishonor others, it is not self-seeking, it is not easily angered, it keeps no record of wrongs. **6** Love does not delight in evil but rejoices with the truth. **7** It always protects, always trusts, always hopes, always perseveres. **8** Love never fails."*

-1 CORINTHIANS 13:4-8

Now, let's replace the word "love" with "coach" and see how that works.

Coach is patient

I believe patience is one of the most underrated qualities of a great coach. It is certainly an underrated quality of a great husband or wife. When patience is present, people are transformed. Patience is an attractive, uncommon quality today.

When you are patient with your players despite them being knuckleheads at times, they feel loved and respected. When someone feels loved and respected by you, you *have* won him or her over. You are now free to have influence in his or her life. *Patience* is a critical part of love-powered coaching. Does your patience need attention?

What about long-term patience? We all know that athletes develop at different speeds. One of the mistakes I made early on a strength coach was getting frustrated when a kid couldn't figure out how to deadlift properly, or when a kid would give less than his best effort even though he had been with us for three months. Through many failures and making kids feel unloved, I got better.

One of my favorite examples of patient coaching is from one of our coaches, Travis. Travis has a way of connecting with athletes that I deeply admire. One kid in particular came to us and was labeled by his basketball coach as "the lazy kid." Travis spent the first month with Brian trying to figure out what made him tick, what frustrated him, what motivated him, what he liked, and what he did not like. Seeking to understand before being understood is something Travis does well. But it is all centered around the idea of patient coaching. We do not need our kids to be motivated, high-performing achievers overnight. Expectations lead to frustration, and that is not love. That is not patience.

Travis begins with the end in mind. If he has an athlete for a three-month window, his objective is to get buy-in by the *end* of those three months. This is wise coaching. Being able to reverse engineer from the end objective is a valuable, necessary practice for any coach who wants to make a lifelong impact.

Where focus goes, energy flows. Patience is a characteristic you can get better at.

Coach is kind

An unkind coach will likely have a funeral someday that zero of his former players attend.

Is it kind to point out all of the things your athlete does wrong in front of other people? Would you like it if your boss at work one day decided to share with your team all the things you stunk at and needed to get better at?

"Carrie continues to let fear hold her back. She is inconsistent with her performance. One day she is motivated, the next she is not. Her anxiety and self-doubt continue to negatively affect her performance." Right in front of you, as if you were not even there, your boss cuts you down.

This is an extreme example, but it's one I have witnessed far too many times between parents and athletes. I had this happen recently when a young tennis "star" came into PFP for her initial evaluation. Before the workout even started, her parents executed the exact situation that happened with Carrie and her boss. Mom would fire a comment about how Grace's anxiety before matches was unbearable to watch. Dad would follow her up with a comment about how Grace never gave more than 80% of her best effort. Back and forth this went on for 10 minutes.

After the evaluation I sat down with the parents. Heart pounding, I knew I needed to address the parent-player issue at hand. If not, the actions of this parent might negatively affect the rest of this young lady's life. If I courageously addressed it with love, I knew my words could positively alter the trajectory of their relationship, and her life.

"Mom, being a sports parent is one of the hardest jobs today. Finding the balance between wanting your daughter to be the best she can be, while also not placing unneeded pressure and expectation on her, is neither easy nor intuitive. However, your daughter needs a break – mentally, physically, and emotionally. Tennis should never be discussed at the dinner table. If *she* does not bring it up, she likely does not want to talk about it. I know you want to help, but your daughter shared with me during the evaluation that she fears disappointing you. She also shared that she feels like the only way you will be proud of her and accept her is if she accomplishes all the things you want her to accomplish in tennis. I think you need to have a vulnerable, humble conversation with her and admit the flaws in your approach."

I waited. I prepared for the mom to grab her keys, grab her daughter, and say, "See ya later."

But that is not what happened. Instead, she looked at me and said, "Thank you for the reminders. Not enough coaches are saying these things. In fact, they are making it worse sometimes."

I smile thinking about how that one courageous moment could change that girl's future. We have the power as coaches and parents to *choose kindness*, even if that means being truthful, honest, and facing the brutal facts of reality. Love speaks truth in a way that builds up but does not condemn.

Coach is not self-seeking

Cutting players at a young age is a controversial topic. Why do you cut players? Is it so that your team *looks better?* An important question to answer is this: is it in the best long-term interest of that young man or woman for you to cut them or to keep them and develop them?

I know this is not a black or white area. But if you are a coach who cuts players because they have bad attitudes, low work ethics, poor communication skills, lack of athleticism, or any other poor qualities, I am going to try to convince you to start keeping them.

A kid's missteps, bad actions, bad decisions, and poor attitudes are *symptoms* of a heart that is out of harmony with the way our hearts were designed to function. And as a coach, *you* have more power than *any other person that ever comes into their life* to change them from the *inside out.* How do you do it? With love.

Coach, you have the power to conduct successful heart surgery. You have the power to operate on the heart of your athletes, and in turn, change the trajectory of the rest of their lives.

When you choose to act out of *love* and keep the players most coaches would otherwise cut, you are being a coach of impact. When you choose to act out of *love* and seek to develop your players who are acting out of line with your desires for them team, you are stewarding your power well.

Cutting players is just one example of how we, as coaches, can be guilty of looking out for the reputation of our team or organization instead of the athletes' best interests. There are many other examples of this.

There was a 12-year-old girl named Tess with whom I did mindset coaching. One day she came in with her mother and told me she was going to quit the team and quit gymnastics altogether.

"Why?" I asked her.

"Yesterday at practice was the final straw. I could not figure out how to stick my landing coming off beam. I was having a bad day at school before that too. I'll admit, I had a bad attitude. My coach was standing on top of some boxes with a pool noodle (those long styrofoam things you use in the pool) coaching me on beam. I fell for the third time in a row and my coach *jumped* off the boxes right in front of me, *slammed* the noodle down on the mats (which sounded like a shotgun) and *yelled*, 'Why can't you get it together? Your attitude has sucked all day! You're never going to make it!'"

Compassion and love sit on the exact opposite side of the table from self-seeking. Luckily, I was able to teach Tess that her *coach* likely had a broken heart. His actions were a result of *his problems,* not hers. He clearly wanted her to do well for his *ego,* for *self-promotion.* He wanted the *team to be the best and to win,* and it came at the expense of a teachable moment where he could have taught Tess any number of valuable lessons. We've all failed here as coaches, but we must recognize that a kid's misdeeds or poor attitude are symptoms of a heart that needs more love. Love wins, coaches. Compassion wins. If you want your players to play better, love them and show compassion for them *where they are.* Seek first to understand, don't seek first a perfect performance.

If we refuse to put the bank account and image of our organization first, and instead do what is in *the athlete's* best interest, everyone will win. We will have the dream team someday and you will have made an incredible impact in the lives of the kids you work with.

As parents, if we refuse to live vicariously through our children, we will be the minority but will also see our children experience peak performance while also maintaining peak levels of joy. We must never let the failures or successes that our athlete experiences on the sports field make us feel too good or too bad about ourselves.

Coach does not envy

To envy means that you desire to have a quality, a possession, or an attribute that belongs to someone else. Envy takes it to another level and is willing to do *anything* to get it, even if that means manipulating, cheating, lying, stealing, or being an imposter.

As a coach, do you ever compare your team to another? Do you ever wish you had another coach's team? If it is happening even inside your mind or heart, it needs to be fixed if you want to be a love-powered coach.

As a parent, do you ever desire for your athlete to have the qualities and attributes of another athlete? Do you wish you had what another parent had? That is envy, and we are all subject to its grip. Envy needs your attention right now so you can figure out how you will acknowledge it, address it, and go to battle against it.

Envy is not love. Love blossoms where it is planted. Love looks at the diamond within and says, "I know what is inside of *you*. *You* are unique, *you* are special. *You* have greatness within you. You do not need what anyone else has in order to reach your full potential."

Love never, ever, ever, *ever* says, "Why can't you be more like him or her?" Because the minute you do that as a coach or parent, you plant an evil seed inside the mind of your kid that eventually grows into the belief that he or she needs what that *other person has* in order to be great.

If your athlete is comparing himself or herself to others, discontent with what they have, dissatisfied with who they are, it might be because of the example they were given.

Envy is a learned behavior.

We need to look within right now as coaches and youth influencers and own up to our mistakes. Not just for ourselves, but also for the kids we serve. I had to do this back in 2013 when I was comparing *my athletes* and *my ability to motivate and influence athletes* to another performance coach in our area. I failed to realize that I was created to serve a type of athlete different from that other coach. I was so focused on what that other coach was doing that I forgot who I was as a coach. Who was *I* meant to serve? *How* was I gifted to motivate and inspire? You have certain qualities as a coach that will allow you to motivate and inspire your kids to greatness. And those qualities are different than mine. I learned that two of mine were:

1) **A steadfast commitment to my values**. God gave me the ability to be steadfast, consistent, and stay true to who I was. I did not realize that was an attractive and motivating quality for youth athletes to see. I guess it is because it is *rare* to find in a coach nowadays.

2) **Vulnerability.** Admitting when I was wrong, when I did not know something, and sharing stories of my past failures, even the embarrassing ones I used to be ashamed of. I realized this was one of the unique gifts I had been given to inspire kids to believe that they were better than their past and that their setbacks were merely setups for comebacks.

Do not envy other coaches or parents. Bloom where you are planted and figure out how to make the best batch of athletes you can with the ingredients you have been given.

And remember, just as history tells us, bad qualities in leaders become bad qualities in their followers. Any bad habit that becomes a part of our character, such as envy, will be passed down to the kids looking to us for an example to follow.

Coach does not boast

Having studied coaches for the past ten years, I have heard *many* coaches talk with excessive pride about their achievements, possessions, and abilities. And the ones who are smart enough not to talk about it end up displaying it in their actions.

I am lucky. God humbled me early on in my coaching career. I found myself bragging about the athletes whom I had trained who went on to earn big college scholarships. God reminded me that I was a *small* part of that. Here is the truth about how important Andrew is to their stories:

The truth is that those college athletes had other coaches and mentors growing up. They had parents who raised them and shaped them into high-performing, confident young leaders. But more importantly, it was *God,* not Andrew, who gave them the *mind and the drive to* want to work hard in the classroom and on the field. I did not plant the *passion* inside them to want to play the sport. I did not give them the *bodies* to perform at a high-level. I do not downplay my impact. I just know that I am fulfilling the assignment God has given me and I am using the tools He has given me to make the impact I have made. I know my place in the story of an athlete making it to the next level now. I am a part of the story, nothing more and nothing less.

When you speak boastfully, your players see it. And just as it happens with envy, your athletes will grow up to be coaches, parents, or teachers who speak in such a way that the spotlight shines on them, even though they do not deserve all the credit. After all, sports are a team thing. As coaches, we are *part* of the team, not *the* team.

"A great leader takes a little more than his share of the blame, and a little less than his share of the credit."
−Arnold H. Glasow

Boasting about your kids

Have you ever heard a parent talk with excessive pride about the happenings of last night's game? "Jody had three goals and two assists."

It's funny. Despite most people not really caring about the results of the game, the parent on the receiving end will say things like, "Oh my goodness, that's amazing! She is the best!"

I think people do that because they are scared to tell a parent the truth, that sports are just a game, and that Suzy's three goals last night may deserve a high five, but they do not deserve boasting about her like she just saved someone's life. There is a *big* reason we must get this right, and we will touch on that later on in the book. However, by making a huge deal about a game with three goals, you are setting your child up for massive self-doubt and disappointment for all the games that she will *fail* to score three goals.

Three goals and two assists is not amazing. We use that word too much. It is honestly not even worth talking about the next day at work. If someone asks, it means they are interested. Goals, assists, scholarships, and whatever other people in our world consider amazing and successful are not worth spotlighting. It is counterculture to think that way, but as you keep reading, you may realize the scary truth about what happens when we continue to boast about achievements.

Remember, it is a sport, a game, and your kid played well. The end.

What IS Amazing?

What *is* amazing, inspiring, and worth talking about is when your kid played horribly, got benched, yet continued to cheer on her teammates and maintain a positive attitude. What is remarkable is when your kid, despite being benched, decided to talk with the coach the next day and ask what she could do better. With self-awareness, your daughter responds to the coach by saying, "I now know why you benched me. I am going to work on that part of my game. Thanks for being a great coach."

That is amazing! That is worth talking about! Why? Because it is inspiring and helpful for *others* to hear. It shines a spotlight on a behavior that can and should be repeated. Your daughter scoring goals and winning is not inspiring for others to hear, especially if the parent on the receiving end hears it, decides that her daughter isn't good enough, and then starts comparing her to the other girls because of it. Then the crazy cycle continues. (Note: it is all about how you say what you say, and *why* you are saying it. Your intent matters.)

Boasting is a big deal. It too deserves your attention and energy to go to battle against it.

Coach does not dishonor others

Would you say that screaming at a kid in the middle of practice and/ or calling them out in front of their teammates is a recipe for positive influence and impact?

Or would you say that as a coach it is in your best interest *and* the best interest of your players for you to *refrain?*

To *refrain* from embarrassing them, *refrain* from calling them out, *refrain* from demeaning them, *to refrain* from sarcastic or rude comments?

Praise in public, condemn in private. Praise the right behaviors and condemn the wrong behaviors, but never, ever, ever condemn the *person*. That is love-powered leadership at its finest. Flex your self-control muscle, Coach. If you are getting worked up over a kid messing up or costing the team success, think back to your failures as a kid. Empathy is a word that comes to mind. Realism is another. Our players are not perfect and should not be treated as if they are. Honor them by always, always, always being a coach who shows them dignity through our own self-control.

When love is fully functioning in you and *through you*, you can become just as influential and impactful as the greatest coaches who have ever walked the planet, such as the late John Wooden. Yes, *just* as impactful and influential. It will simply require more intention and effort on our part as coaches, a bigger focus on executing a "love-coaching game plan" day in and day out.

Coach is not easily angered

I know this one will hit home with a lot of us. The busier you are in your personal and professional life, the more easily angered you are. The lower your emotional and mental capacities, the quicker you are to get angry with your athletes.

Isn't it odd how some coaches can sit back on the sidelines and refrain from outbursts, even as their team makes mistakes, while other coaches will flip their hands into the air, spout out a curse word, and crash down into their seat if a player simply misses a free throw? It is not odd if you realize that a coach's uncontrolled temper is always a result of what is going on in their life *outside of the sport itself.*

Love never places unrealistic, cruel expectations on others, and therefore coaches who love do not get easily angered. May I submit for your consideration that maybe the unrealistic expectations you have for your players, co-workers, or family members could be a root cause of your short fuse and frustration with them?

Coach John Wooden knew this well. He knew as the *leader* that when his players messed up during a game, it was at least part his fault. He also knew that mistakes would happen and that his players *would* do the wrong thing despite knowing better (don't we all do that?). And he gave grace in those moments. After all, if his players were perfect, he would become obsolete.

Don't we all know that screaming from the sideline as a coach *or* parent only creates fear, doubt, and frustration in your players? We all know that there is no person on this planet that performs better when he or she is fearful or frustrated. If we know it, why do we still do it?

Unrealistic expectations. They are cruel, they are unhelpful, and you would never want others to place them on you.

Be slow to anger as a coach. Slow to speak out of frustration. *Identify* when the feelings are surfacing, then refrain. Watch what happens. And if you feel like you are in a season of life where you are becoming easily angered by anyone and anything that goes wrong, take a step back and fill up *your* emotional bucket.

How are *you* doing, coach? Really, how are you? Do you need to create some margin in your life? Go on a walk in nature. Meditate. Do yoga. Take a vacation. Take something off your plate! Do whatever you need to do to overcome the anger issue. Start taking care of you by putting a weekly (or daily) appointment in your calendar to take time for some solitude, renewal, rejuvenation, relaxation, and so on.

Coaches are killing the confidence of our athletes because they cannot control their anger. Love is the only worthy opponent that can defeat anger.

Bonus: Coach disciplines

> *"Leadership is not about making people happy,*
> *it is about making them better."*
> -- JOHN C. MAXWELL

Love does not mean you lay down and do whatever it takes to appease your athlete. This is known as a "friend-coach," a parent or coach who has insecurities and tries to be cool for their kids, one who cares more about being popular than they do about being respected. They get the order wrong. Friend comes second.

Love does discipline. Have you ever heard about the biblical story when Jesus flipped over tables and drove out the moneychangers when he saw that they were using the *house of prayer* to sell goods and make a selfish profit? The lesson we can learn as love-centered coaches is that this was *carefully planned and thought through in advance* by "Coach Jesus." He did not flip the tables reactively out of anger, temper, or frustration, but rather he did so out of *love*. He knew that this is how he needed to address to situation to show the magnitude of the problem. Selfish ambitions and the love of money was the root of all evil, so Jesus needed to give the appropriate attention to the situation.

Have a plan for how you will respond, react, and discipline your athletes when they:

- Talk back
- Disrespect you, the refs, the opponents, or a teammate
- Mess up in school

All the different scenarios are worth thinking through and planning out *how* you will love through discipline.

Bonus #2: Coach refrains from using coercive power

Loyalty is something most coaches want from their players. You want them to be loyal to you, to their teammates, to your philosophies, to the game plan, and to the goals of the team.

But the problem is that far too many coaches and parents nowadays are using threats to get their athletes to do things the way they want them done, threats such as "running punishment if you do not do this and that right during the game." This type of power abuse *never* creates reliable or trustworthy players.

Coercive power: the use of force, might, or strength to threaten, intimidate, or punish someone who does not choose to comply with your will. Coercive power is used when a coach or parent lacks the ability to influence a player and gain their trust and respect. Love-powered leadership is the answer.

Our coaches at PFP are obsessed with the idea of being servant-leaders. It sounds silly and simple, but we regularly talk about how to be "nicer" to our athletes. We know that these kids come to us by *choice,* and that we are there to *serve them,* not be *served by them.* Do you want to know what the result of servant-leadership is? Kids beg their parents to come back to us.

Guess what they are coming to do? Our athletes come to us to workout. Exercise. Lift weights. They are *choosing* to come to do the thing that almost *nobody likes to do!* Why? Because our coaches *never use coercive power.* We never give an arbitrary punishment for a kid who messes up their squat form or does 10 reps instead of 12. We know that if a kid does the wrong thing, they need to be coached up and *shown* how to do it better.

On the inside, most kids are crying out, "Coach, will you please *show me how to do it better,* rather than *telling me that I did it wrong and then insisting that I do it better?"*

What about when a kid purposefully does the wrong thing, skips out on a set, quits early, or is disrespectful towards a coach? Is coercive power appropriate then?

No, it's not. Not if you want buy-in and impact. When a kid intentionally does the wrong thing, there is a *reason why!* He or she has an infection of thought or an infection in their heart. They may come from a home with abuse, poor leadership, or lack of discipline. They may have *never been shown unconditional love and respect.* Maybe they have never had a great role model.

Seek first to understand, then to be understood.

Instead of lashing out at that kid, giving them an arbitrary punishment, and giving them a reason to resent you, choose to *love them where they are.* I can speak out against coercive power because I've royally messed this up many times. I once told a young female lacrosse player not to do cross country because it would slow her down on the lacrosse field. She told me that she liked cross country and that it was good for her mind. I told her it was a bad idea and the tone of my voice clearly sent the message to her that she was not very smart and was making a terrible decision. The girl left in tears that day and did not come back through our doors for a full year after that. I had to work hard to restore and reconcile the relationship. That is what happens when you try to use your power to coerce someone into making a decision *you feel is right for them.* The best coaches teach their athletes how to make the right decisions, they don't make them for them.

When I learned about servant leadership from studying the life of Jesus, I changed my ways. And when I did, my influence with athletes multiplied.

Punishment is not a bad thing. We just want to be sure that the punishment fits the crime, and that as a coach or parent, you kneel down in front of your athletes and lovingly explain *why.* If you can't make time to explain the why, prepare to be forced to make time to correct bigger problems later.

How does running suicides as a result of dropping passes in a game make any logical sense? If your athletes dropped passes in a game, should you not spend more time on hand-eye coordination drills, and passing and catching drills? At the very least, have them run a sprint and then immediately transition into catching when they are tired.

A quick way to lose your players' loyalty towards you is to confuse them with punishment. If you want to cause your players to play with the *fear of messing up,* give them a painful punishment *if they mess up during the game. That* will elicit a strong fear response.

Imagine if your boss told you that for every sales call that you did not close, you were going to have to kneel on rice at your desk for 10 minutes per call. This is known as Chinese torture. You would be so nervous on those phone calls that you would never be able to concentrate on the person's pain points, desires, or other things you need to know to close the sale. Your focus would be on rice rather than relationships.

All of this goes back to a coach or parent, knowingly or unknowingly, exercising coercive power.

Love, on the other hand, operates under the law of liberty. When your athletes feel like they have freedom, when they feel like their opinion matters, and when they feel like you truly care about what is best for them, they will reward you with loyalty. Loyalty is earned, always.

Ask yourself, have I been using coercive power? What do I need to do to change?

Chapter 15

LIFE TRANSFORMING COACH

The primary responsibility of a love-powered coach is to properly assess your player's mental, physical, and emotional state, come up with a diagnosis based on their symptoms, and prescribe a plan of action that is going to address their *biggest* problems. That plan of action may be outsourcing certain things to other professionals, but it is your job to recognize that there *are* problems. Don't ignore them and chalk it up as "normal."

The first step to becoming a life-transforming coach is to decide what is best for the athlete right now. Unfortunately as a coach, what is best for the athlete is often not the easiest or most convenient option for *you*.

Imagine you come across a young male lacrosse player who has no father figure, struggles with false confidence, bottles up and suppresses his emotions, and has trouble shooting with his left hand. What is the most important thing that you want to help him with?

Addressing the weak left hand without coming up with a game plan to help him mentally and emotionally is like the doctor who ignored the cancer and prescribed a stool softener.

I was guilty of this for six years as a coach. As I mentioned earlier, we once had an athlete who had been cutting herself for three months without me or any other coaches noticing. Yes, the self-harm was right in front of our faces. I was so focused on the *external* problems that I couldn't even see the pain on the *inside.*

I was so focused on improving her forehand *strength* that I didn't even recognize the forearm *marks.* Can you guess what *she* cared about more? Do you think *she* wanted to improve her shot more than her broken heart?

NO!

I do not think you need to have 10 years of coaching experience before you begin noticing what *really* matters most. As I mentioned in the beginning, you just need to begin *viewing yourself differently.* Are you a softball coach or are you a loving, life-transforming coach?

A great exercise is to imagine yourself at your own funeral and all the athletes you ever worked with are standing on stage telling the stories about how you impacted them. I want you to write down all of the things you want them to say about how you helped them.

Would they say, "Coach Andrew helped transform my jump shot in 11th grade, which in turn helped me become the loving, patient, present father I am today for my kids?"

Probably not. Think about that for a while and write it down. Beginning with the end in mind is a proven way to ensure that your life's work as a coach is purpose driven and accurately focused.

Coaching myth: "What the parent wants, the parent gets. I am there to serve the parent's desires for their kid."

Despite knowing Corey's biggest needs were stretching, recovery, and injury prevention, I allowed his overbearing parents whose primary concerns were a higher vertical jump to dictate my coaching game plan. I didn't want them to get mad and stop bringing Corey in for workouts, but I also knew that higher vertical required a lot more strength training and power training (two things that will be counter-productive for an athlete in season).

The result of bending to the parents' wishes? Corey experienced more injury, less enthusiasm for basketball, and resentment toward me!

Coach, stand your ground. Be steadfast. If you know your ways are true, good, and long-term focused, communicate that to the parents and stand firm. You can still throw in a box jump or two to appease the parent if they just won't let it go.

Remember, leadership is not about making people happy, it is about making them better. It is tough sometimes, but leaders do tough things. I think the hardest part is when societal pressures rise and there is no win-win scenario. You cannot always do what is in the best interest of your athletes *and* please all parties involved.

If you do not have the right training and are unsure of how to go about helping a young male or female with challenges outside of just their sport skills, I suggest you commit now to going on a journey to learn.

Anxiety that comes from the fear of rejection and not being accepted is more important to address than getting your player's 300-yard shuttle time to go from one minute and ten seconds down to one minute. A mental breakthrough often impacts a player's on-field performance more than that ten-second drop anyway.

I am not saying ignore the conditioning, but what I am saying is that you as a coach have the power to alter the trajectory of the next 65 years of a young man or woman's life. We need to check our practice plan, literally.

Chapter 16

EQUIPPING AND EMPOWERING

Some coaches are so technically smart and great at giving advice that they create athletes that *really* depend on them. If your goal is to create *dependent* athletes, this is good. But if you have faced the reality that you will *no longer be here*, than maybe your goal is similar to mine – to create athletes who *can always count on and* depend on you but know how to succeed *independent from you.*

Eventually you will not be there. Eventually your athletes will need to spread their wings and fly without you. Have you given them the tools they need to succeed on their own? This is called *equipping*. If you haven't, Part 4 is going to blow your mind and challenge you to go deeper, something most people are scared to do today.

In 2018, I found myself to be guilty of being a "teller coach." I have always been an obsessive learner – books, conferences, workshops, online courses, you name it. I know I have spent more money on postgraduate education than I did in college. Combine that with having many great mentors who I constantly go to for advice, and you get a head full of knowledge that if not tamed, can turn into word vomit as I "tell" my athletes all the right answers to their problems.

One day I texted my mentor, Steve, and asked him for his advice on a decision I needed to make. His response forever changed the way I coach people and operate my *own life.*

"Andrew, what are your values?" my mentor asked.

I shared with him my top three values, the most important things in my life, the things that defined who I believed God wanted me to become and the direction He wanted to take my life.

"Ok. If you decide to go through with this, where does *that* fit into those values? Will it require you to sacrifice a top three value for one that might not even crack the top ten? Is this a *right now* project for you to pursue, or a *later on* project?"

He continued to *ask questions* that helped me to come to the conclusion *on my own*. He taught me how to think through a decision-making process. This is a key to love-powered coaching. It is so simple, but few do it. Asking the right questions is more powerful than giving the right answers. Teaching, not telling, is the name of the game if you want to create athletes who can depend on you to learn how to be independent from you!

If you are like me, you are confident giving advice and having all the answers. Be careful not to get addicted to it like I was. I think we need to have more of these conversations:

Athlete: "Coach, what do you think I should do?"

Coach: "I could tell you, but I believe you know the right thing to do. You have been given instincts for a reason. Listen to them. What is your gut telling you?"

Some situations obviously require counsel and advice. The gut isn't *always* firing on all cylinders, especially as a teenager. But in general, our youth influencers need to aim to build *decision-making muscles* in the students we work with. It is similar to me watching my seven-month-old son, Jack, try to pick up pieces of egg and put them into his mouth. I let him go at it for a few minutes until eventually, I step in and show him how to do it. Jack needs to eat, but it is not pertinent that it happens *immediately*. Letting him learn by *trying* and *failing* is important.

Even if it is a longer process and more inconvenient for you, encouraging your kids to *think through decisions* is important. The next level is teaching them how to make decisions based on their values. Ultimately, this is what we do when we give them advice, right? We project our values onto them and their situation and share with them what *we* would do based on our experience and values.

Another thing we can do is to teach them about delayed gratification versus quick fixes so they can see clearly when they are about to make a decision that feels good *now* but will bite them later. When I get to the end of my life, "equipper and empowerer" are two words I want to describe the type of coach and leader that I was. I believe these are the marks of a love-powered coach and one who will impact many people on a deeper level.

Chapter 17

STAND IN THE GAP, CHANGE A LIFE

Stephanie's Story

In 2016, we started training a young teenage athlete named Stephanie. Everything about her is awesome. She is the kind of girl every coach dreams of working with – mature, hard-working, kind, funny, caring.

We worked with her on and off for about a year to help her improve her strength, speed, and mindset for softball. But because she lived about an hour away from our facility, she had to stop training when school started again.

It was the winter of 2017 when tragedy struck. Her father passed away suddenly after a morning workout. It absolutely crushed her and her family.

She and her dad used to work out together three days a week at 6:00 a.m. – yes, a middle schooler going to the gym willingly at 6:00 a.m., three days a week before class. At the time, work was crazy for me. But I felt God nudging me to connect with her.

What I am about to say is mission critical. I didn't question God about my next move. I didn't think about it. I didn't ask my wife. I didn't calculate the fact that it would require me leaving my house at 4:30 a.m. to get to the gym by 6:00.

"Steph, I cannot begin to tell you how sorry I am. Do you want to work out together tomorrow morning?"

That one text message to her started a weekly workout where we would train together, talk, connect, and reflect. I was able to mentor her and help her through the storm. Why did God want me to drive 90 minutes every week to do this?

For one, I've been called to coaching. Called to mentoring. It's in my top five core values for my life, and therefore, I prioritize it.

I have learned to own my role of being a *role model*. In 2016 I made a big, intentional decision that I would take ownership of the fact that God chose me to be a leader and a role model to many teenage and college aged kids.

For some coaches, they feel the weight of that responsibility and the result can be dread or the fear of not being enough. Some coaches *accept* the responsibility. But love-powered coaches have a different mindset. They own it and choose to stand in the gap, no matter what it takes.

The second reason I believe I was called to drive to West Virginia for weekly workouts with her was because God, in His infinite wisdom, had perfectly ordained for these "appointments" to happen. He knew what was lurking in the future for my dad, for my family. He didn't force me to do it, but He gave me the opportunity. Steph was able to help *me* during the storm I went through with my dad. I was able to better relate with her and understand her as a result of my dad's passing.

I believe one of the biggest reasons you and I have been called to Love Powered Leadership is so that we can *stand in the gap*. There is a gap between where the people currently are and where they could be – where they are *supposed to be.*

A kid you work with has a strained relationship with his mother. Will you stand in the gap? Will you do whatever you can to help bridge that gap?

A kid you work with has body image issues. They lack self-esteem, and more than anything else, they *want* to feel good about themselves. Will you stand in the gap?

Someone you coach has ADHD and cannot concentrate on a task for more than 10 minutes. They try to sit and do homework for an hour because they do not know any better. They are failing classes and need a new strategy. They need to start blocking time and only going at it for 20 minutes a clip. Will you stand in the gap? Will you be the one to help them with their time management?

Maybe you do not have all the answers to your kids' problems. But you can do three things:

1. **Learn.** Become better yourself so you can teach them. Parts 3 and 4 will teach you how to be a mindset coach.

2. **Outsource it.** You may not have the water, but you can lead them to it.

3. **Listen and empathize.** Sometimes all that love requires of you in the moment is to wholeheartedly, with both ears, listen and feel what they feel.

There is never a bad time to mentor, coach, and connect one on one with another person. As the saying goes, "There is never a wrong time to do the right thing."

Chapter 18

THE TWO MOST POWERFUL WORDS: "COACH SAYS"

Abuse, Misuse, or Refuse to Use Your Power

Jeff Duke, creator of 3Dimensional Coaching, says that two of the most powerful words in the life of a 21st century adolescent are "Coach says."

Billy Graham said it this way: "A coach will impact more people in one year than the average person does in a lifetime."

I have found that many coaches are either abusing, misusing, or refusing to use their power for good.

What is the most common phrase that athletes go home and say? "But mom, coach said _____."

This is proof enough that you have power – massive power. If you are reading this, I doubt you *abuse* your power. I also doubt that you *refuse to use* your power. But I can guarantee you may be *misusing* your power by not leveraging it for the best of your athletes.

When you sit your athletes down for 15 minutes before practice and do a mental-game writing exercise that helps them work on their values and vision for their future (go to www.andrewjsimpson.com/book-insider to access the Values and Vision Exercise), you are using your power as a coach for good. You get to determine the practice schedule and how you spend your time with your athletes. That power alone is immense.

When you schedule a one-on-one meeting two times per year with each of your athletes and have an intentional "game plan" to help them have personal breakthroughs, you are using your power for good. During that meeting, when you really dive deep and seek to understand the state of your athlete's heart, you could alter the trajectory of the rest of that kid's life. What you say or don't say matters. Remember, kids place a premium value on the opinions of their coaches.

Terry's Story

Terry is a 17-year-old male who is battling depression, anxiety, and very low self-esteem. One evening, I happened to have one free hour in my schedule from 3:00-4:00 p.m. His dad was driving him from school back to their house when all of the sudden, Terry freaked out. He was coming down off of his depression medication because it was causing adverse effects. That is when Terry looked at his dad dead in the eyes and said six words that no parent ever wants to hear from their child.

"I won't be alive tomorrow morning."

His dad was at a loss for words and did not know what to do. He drove to PFP. From the parking lot Terry's dad called us and said, "Andrew, will you please come out to the car. Terry is not in good shape. I don't know where else to go."

I spent the next hour and a half talking with Terry, listening to his cry for help, and hugging him. By the end of our 90 minutes together, Terry was smiling, laughing, and far more joyful. Between the PFP team and myself, we have taken him under our wing and are working hard to build him back up. He gets mentally beaten down by immature kids and school and a society that values a bunch of things he has not been given. Therefore, we must build him up every time we see him.

That night I could not get to sleep. I thought to myself, "How many other kids are out there struggling to fit in, feeling unloved and rejected, but are really good at hiding it? How many kids could benefit from a one-on-one lunch with their coach every couple of months? All of them, of course."

I used to attempt to put the weight of the world on my shoulders. I used to ask God for stronger shoulders thinking He would provide and then I could help everyone. I learned the hard way. I no longer believe that bearing the burdens of *every* kid's problem is wise. Now I work to build up other love-powered coaches to share the burden.

I know my power as a coach. I want God to look me in the eyes as I enter Heaven and say, "Well done, good and faithful servant. You used the power I gave you *wisely*."

You get to decide how much is too much as a love-powered coach. You get to choose to *use your power* and to meet with Terry *before* Terry freaks out. **You must look beyond the physical and into the hearts and souls of these young men and women.** They have stories. They have struggles. And while you alone cannot save them, you can use what you have been given to *help them.* The Golden Rule is a staple of a love-powered coach.

Chapter 19

IF NOT YOU, WHO?

The athlete on your team who has no father figure, has a learning disability, or has lost a sibling tragically – if you don't step up and take responsibility as that young man or woman's mentor, who will?

The reality we all have to face as coaches is that *we are the only person that we can 100% depend on to come alongside of a kid in need.*

"I need family balance."

"My other job is demanding more of me."

God wants you and me to let go of control, stop over-calculating everything, stop aiming for some ideal life with perfect work-life balance, and be radically obedient to His calling for you to serve that kid in need.

I also believe God wants us to *stop* trying to replace one-to-one personal connection with technology. Leveraging my time through group coaching or mentoring is great, but it does not replace the need for one-to-one connection. It only complements it.

Every coach needs to decide, "Am I a baseball coach or a life-transforming mentor?"

Am I a 4:00-6:00 p.m. coach *or* is this my purpose in life?

Do I really need to be serving my athletes less *or* do I need to do a better job of communicating to my husband/wife and family that God is calling me to serve these kids right now?

I didn't say to my wife, "Hey Daniela, I want to work out with this athlete once a week. But I know it's 90 minutes away and you and I like to do our Bible study and devotional together those days. What do you think? It's pretty far. I could think of another option. Would you rather I stayed home?"

Instead I said, "Daniela, God is talking to me. He is saying I need to be there for her right now. One day a week only. We will make it up by doing our devotional in the evening that day. Is that OK with you? If not, let's talk about it."

I know it is a tricky balance. But if you are like me, you can be more intentional about the balancing act, more intentional with your boundaries and communication.

I tell my wife all the time, "If not me, who?"

And she supports it. She believes what I believe, that God has called me to serve outside of the nine-to-five, that if a kid needs me to drive two hours to work out with them one or two days a week at 5:00 a.m. because they just lost the most important person in their life, I'm going to do it without hesitation. "Stand in the gap, Andrew. Stand in the gap."

I've missed chip shots. Layups. I've hesitated and justified not standing in the gap. And more times than not, I've regretted it. You don't have to agree with me, but you do have to pick your answer to the question, "If not me, then who?"

Love-powered coaching goes above and beyond. When you go above and beyond the call of duty, your kids notice. It might be 10 years before Stephanie ever takes action as a result of me going above and beyond for her. But I know she won't forget it. The hope and possibility that another life will be positively impacted down the road by Stephanie is enough of a reason for me to continue going above and beyond the call of duty. Remember, the feedback loop on youth influence is long, but worth it. The circle of mentoring is beautiful. We have the opportunity to do it right and create ripple effects with an endless impact.

Chapter 20

FUN, LOVE, AND INSPIRATION: THE FOUNDATION FOR UNSTOPPABLE GROWTH

"Fun is one of the most important — and underrated — ingredients in any successful venture."

-- RICHARD BRANSON

The foundation for everything we do as coaches is the following: fun, love, and inspiration.

If you pull back the curtains on every aspect of our program, you'll find one of those things at the root.

Why FUN?

Sports and being physically active are a choice. They are *optional*. You don't *have* to do it.

I've surveyed many great coaches and the ones who are making the biggest difference in their athletes' lives are the ones who are intentional about creating a fun, joy-filled environment in which their athletes can grow. The most successful coaches also make sure *they* have fun along the way.

I was at an event recently where Drew Brees came and spoke. He was asked the question, "Drew, you are 40 years old. How are you still playing? Why are you still playing?"

Drew's response: "I still love the game of football. Last season was possibly the *most fun* I have ever had. That's a big reason I am coming back. It started at the top with Coach Payton making it fun. He *created* fun in the locker room."

Drew went on to talk about his teammates and how every single one of them had fun, positive attitudes. They all worked hard and hung out together.

I find that response so insightful for us. So many kids are burning out from sports. Drew says it is because sports become "too serious too quick." I agree.

People will not do things that they do not *have* to do for long if they do not *enjoy* them.

Because of this truth about our youth, we intentionally make our gym fun so that kids have the desire to play sports and work out long after they no longer "have to." Once you reach 18 years old, sports are not really required to feel like you fit in. That's why so many athletes stop playing, even recreationally, after high school.

Let me say that again. One of our main objectives as youth fitness and/or sports coaches should be for our athletes to *want to* participate in sports and fitness when they no longer *have to.*

What are some ways to make it fun without diminishing the other objective?

It starts with the people. Who are you? Who is on your coaching team? Are you fun, goofy, light-hearted people who take their jobs seriously but do not take themselves too seriously? This is who we hire at PFP. Our fifth core value is *"Work Hard, Play Hard: we take our jobs seriously, but do not take ourselves too seriously."*

We play tug of war, tag, and other games to create fun warm-ups. We systematically plant jokes into our motivational messages when appropriate.

We aim to make the experience *fun* so that our students *want* to come back. It sounds simple, but one of the ways we measure our success by how many kids we have in our doors that have a desire to be there. This objective dictates everything we do as coaches. Their parents could force them, but I personally hate that. Making it fun so they want to come back does two important things:

1. **It gives us more time to mentor them *and* their parents.** Sometimes it isn't until a year later that a kid opens up and is open to the type of transformational coaching that will change his or her life. Parents also appreciate the mentoring we give them on how to be better sports parents.

2. **A fun, positive association with sports training and fitness instills a desire inside them to be physically fit and active for life.** If, at a young age, they begin associating exercise with fun, they will be more likely to continue working out when they get older.

"When you have your health, you have a thousand dreams. When you do not have your health, you have one dream." The vision we have is to see all of the kids we work with go on to live healthy, fit, active lives and to value their health and fitness as adults. Making their teenage experience with fitness *fun* is a key element to achieving this outcome.

Why INSPIRATION?

We all know that kids are capable of far more than they believe they are. And because they don't *believe* they can do things, their actions follow their beliefs.

Like you, we aim to pull the best out of our students every single day, which typically requires getting them slightly outside of their comfort zones.

"Today you are going to do 10 chin-ups."

"WHAT! I can't do that!"

"Yes you can, and we are going to do it together. One rule: do not give up. You've got this."

And so we create opportunities for them to prove to *themselves* that they are able. They are capable. They have way more in their tank than they ever knew. "You are able. You are capable. Now repeat that to yourself, John. Believe it. It's true."

We call this *increasing capacity.* Once you push yourself further than you thought you could go (physically *or* mentally) you have just increased your capacity. It is a beautiful thing.

We all need to be inspired. We all need someone to tell us and show us that they believe we have more inside of us than we are currently accessing.

Why LOVE?

Two reasons.

The first is that it is the deepest longing we all have – to be loved and accepted, unconditionally.

It is for this reason that we have such a wide diversity of students. We have those with little athletic ability as well as high-level D1 athletes. Everyone is accepted and loved by our team and our other guests. You do not have to look a certain way, have a certain set of skills, or accomplish or achieve *anything* to be viewed as special and worthy by our team.

Accomplishments and accolades are great, but we do not value those things above character and effort. We believe that when character and effort are rewarded, the accolades are a natural by-product.

The second reason that love is foundational is because students aren't getting enough of it, especially in the sports world.

As their mentor-leaders, we define "love" as *doing* the following things for our athletes:

1. Being patient and understanding with them when they are angry, frustrated, or not "feelin' it."

2. Serving them – helping them clean up weights, get water for them, stretch them.

3. Showing up to visit them when they are injured or struggling with a "life storm."

4. Reaching out to them weekly via video or text.

5. Having secret high fives.

6. *Pushing* them to do more, never allowing them to settle for an average effort, and then taking the time to explain *why.*

7. One-on-one connection time with them no matter how many there are – we all need this. Love sacrifices.

8. Never comparing them to someone else.

9. Helping them through decision-making processes, sports-related or not.

FUN.

INSPIRATION.

LOVE.

We call these *Foundations*. What are yours? Every organization needs a philosophy, a foundation on which to train your team and build upon. I will encourage these three to be a part of yours if you want to maximize your impact as a love-powered coach.

Summary of Part 2:
Love Powered Leadership Principles

- In all situations, a love powered coach must ask, "What does love require of me right now?" It may not always be what you want, but it's always the best long-term play.

- Fear of what others might think about us, our teams, or our players will lead to selfish decisions as a coach.

- John Wooden, arguably the greatest coach of all time, stated that the biggest mistake he made was leaving the word "love" out of the Pyramid of Success.

- Touching the heart is the doorway to influence with your players. Unconditional love is the vehicle to get there.

- Where are you placing conditions on loving your athletes? Conditional love is cruel and helps no one get better.

- 1 Corinthians 13:4-8. Replace the word "love" with "coach," and take an audit of how you are doing. Are you being patient, kind, selfless, humble? Are you being boastful, self-seeking, or easily angered?

- Love disciplines. Love builds a relationship and trust that allows you to be real with your athlete and call them on their shortcomings at appropriate times.

- Love does not use power to lead. Coercive power works in the short term but leads to long-term resentments.

- Don't fall into the parent-pleasing trap. Embrace the uncomfortable conversations and speak your truth to them in love. Love doesn't lie or avoid confrontation.

- Love-powered coaches equip and empower their athletes. Lead them in such a way that they make good decisions and come to their own conclusions. Don't be a "teller coach."

Part 3

TRAINING THE MIND

Chapter 21

MINDSET MATTERS MORE

Melissa's Story

During the summer of 2016, I had an awakening. I received a disturbing phone call from a parent during the middle of the day while I was in my office. Ironically, I was writing a workout program for one of our athletes.

On the other end of the phone was a mother in panic.

"ANDREW! You need to help her. She is falling apart. I think she is at her wit's end with volleyball. I know I am at MY wit's end with watching her unravel and fall apart mentally during games. She gets in her own head after messing up or when coach pulls her out, and after that happens it is all downhill. Do you know of any good sports psychologists?"

After adjusting my mind to the severity of this mother's concern, I had 4,000 thoughts run through my mind.

I thought to myself, "Melissa? Really? She is a rock star. She's a 4.0 student, phenomenal athlete, 25-inch vertical. College prospect. Are we talking about the same person?"

We continued this conversation for a good half hour. This mother was a wreck. *Everything* she had done for Melissa to succeed up to this point seemed to be a waste.

The private hitting coaches. The club team she was paying three grand a year for and spending 20 hours a week driving her to. The strength training and fitness coaches she was paying for.

And then, a few profound ideas dawned on me.

Who tries to fix an engine problem with a new steering wheel cover?

In Part 2, we dove deep into the "emotional health" of our youth. Love-powered leadership has the biggest impact on *that* dimension of health and development.

Part 3 is more about the mind. And through our research, we have found that most parents and coaches are trying to fix *mindset* problems with *physical* solutions.

Your athlete is having trouble managing frustrations on the court? She can't overcome a mistake quickly and therefore that mistake follows her for the next three plays?

She must need more volleyball practice.

It sounds pretty dumb when you put it that way, right?

But that is exactly what we do. There are two sayings we use often that apply to everyone. They are:

1. **Mindset matters more.** *(This includes heart health and spiritual health. "Mindset matters more" just has a better ring to it.)*

2. **MP5:** Mental Preparation Precedes Peak Physical Performance

These two truths are ignored by or unknown to most athletes and coaches. Athletes all over the world are trying to muscle their way to success, literally. But the proof that mindset matters more to athletes and parents shows up in how parents react to the challenges their kids face. When their kid fails to score a goal, they get upset. When their kid self-sabotages and becomes a head case on the court, the parent *freaks!* That is proof that mindset matters *more*.

Here are a few reasons why we many parents and coaches are spinning their wheels, trying to solve *mindset challenges with physical remedies.*

Reason #1: Parents and coaches do not realize that mindset solutions exist and have benefit extensions.

In 2016, when we launched our Mindset Performance Coaching Program, we had *a lot* of learning to do. We also had a lot of *educating* to do. We needed to make parents and coaches aware of the fact that there was this thing called "mindset coaching," and that it was the greatest thing since sliced bread.

Eventually, after so many athletes had experienced true confidence transformation, we hit a tipping point, and word about Mindset Performance Coaching began to travel fast.

Social proof took over and not *as much* education was needed in our gym. However, outside of our four walls, the majority of parents and coaches do not realize that there is a better way. There are Mindset Solutions to fix the Mindset Problems.

It is gut-wrenching to know that so many influencers have not discovered solutions to the real problems their kids are facing. Most have also never found real pathways that lead from current circumstances to peak potential and performance.

Most simply have no clue where to start. Therefore, they conform. They send their kid to the camps that the other parents send their kids to. They hire the hitting coach. They get the trainer.

They just keep piling on more and more stuff to enhance their child's *physical performance.*

Benefit Extensions

The fantastic thing about training the mind is that typically there is an overflow of benefits into other areas of a kid's life. If you help an athlete develop a better shot, it only benefits him on the field.

Contrast that to teaching your student-athlete how to overcome mistakes quicker and watch what happens in the classroom after a failed test, or how they respond when they make a mistake in a friendship.

Mindset coaching is a better way to spend your time as a coach. It is not always easy, but it is without a doubt a more comprehensive and holistic approach for the comprehensive, holistic kids that you work with.

Reason #2: Physical solutions are easier.

The second reason why we try to solve Mindset Challenges with Physical Solutions is because it is easier.

This, to the detriment of our youth, unfortunately lines up well with our habitual actions as a society. Stressed? Grab a glass of wine. Headaches? Ibuprofen. Child is acting up? We stick an iPad in their face. These *expedient choices* that we make that are designed to just *get us through the day* are creating horrendous examples for our youth to follow.

When I realized I was doing this, I realized I was being a negligent coach. As a "sports performance guy," I was wired to believe that making an athlete bigger, faster, and stronger was all I needed to do. Satisfy the parent's wants, get the athletes what they *think* they want, and ignore the long-term character shaping and habit building. In other words, ignore the hard, meaningful work.

Sprinkle in a little "mental toughness training," and you are good to go.

Side note: *Mental toughness **training** has been dumbed down by many coaches to be as simple as making a kid puke by pushing him so far outside of his comfort zone that he never wants to work out or play sports again. Mental toughness means so much more than comfort zone training.*

The truth is that this is so much easier to market to parents. Most parents eat this stuff up. Most performance coaches, club coaches, and private specialists are manipulating and feeding into these false promises.

"Vertical jump increases by six inches in six weeks? Sign my kid up!"

In 2016, I noticed that there was a shift ready to happen, and that we as coaches needed to be at the forefront of it. I asked God many times, "Which direction do *you* want the business to go? What kind of stuff do you want us to teach our athletes? What do *you* value most? What should our marketing be about?"

The response I received was that what people today want *most* is real, honest, authentic truth from the people they do business with. This includes their coaches. People are craving love, acceptance, and inspiration more than ever because of the type of crazy, judgmental comparison trap world we live in.

And I have found over the past few years that consumers are way more educated than ever before. They do not fall for the "magical pill," quick fix, microwave mentality promises like they used to.

So over the next two years, our team set out on a journey to better understand the real challenges that our athletes were facing. We stopped taking the path so commonly traveled by coaches and youth influencers and we began a new journey.

We read countless books, watched many videos, and learned from many professionals about how to do *mindset training.*

We studied sports psychology. We studied modern psychology. We learned about the new drives for human motivation. We learned how to teach a student-athlete to overcome adversity. How to get out of their own head and *why* they get in their head to begin with!

We learned ways to teach them how to overcome procrastination, how to restore joy for sports and life, and why they lose their drive and joy to begin with! We learned how to empower and inspire youth athletes to want to be leaders, how to teach in such a way that real, life-long transformation occurs. How to escape the comparison trap, overcome the perfectionist mentality, get past deep-rooted insecurities, and how to stop their pursuit of pleasing everyone at the expense of their own sanity.

We sought answers to those questions. These were the most important questions our athletes and parents had, but were not quite sure how to articulate them.

What was the result of this shift?

We were able to begin providing solutions to the problems rather than just sets, reps, skills, and drills.

Training the mind is *not* as simple as sports psychology.

In fact, we don't even go there until we understand where the athlete is mentally *and* emotionally first. Trying to put sports psychology tricks into a kid's mind who is burnt out from sports and ready to quit is like trying to put the brand new Apple IOS operating system into a 1990 Macintosh computer. It won't compute.

Techniques and tactics to "get in the zone and perform better under pressure" are such a small, small piece of our Mindset Performance Coaching Program. That is why I am so excited to share with you our Insider Resources we provide to you for picking up this book. You will find the private link throughout as you continue reading.

You may not agree, but as love-powered coaches, we strive to help our athletes in uncommon ways for a coach by helping them with *common challenges* like their relationship struggles, how to deal with loss, finances, and time management. Compartmentalization is a bad strategy to develop a highly confident, successful student-athlete. To think that you can focus on just one dimension of a person, ignore all the others, and help someone reach their full potential is silly, isn't it?

Finally, that brings us to the last reason we seek physical solutions for mental challenges.

Reason #3: We are not aware, or we do not want to *admit,* that our kids need to work on their mental and emotional game more than their physical game.

I do not want to make this sound as severe as a drinking problem, a gambling problem, or something major like that, but I don't really know any other way to put it.

Temper Tantrums

Kids who can't manage their frustrations and emotions on the sports field are going to grow up to be husbands and wives who have trouble managing their frustrations in the home.

Burnout

Kids who are burnt out from sports but continue playing just to make mom and dad happy, or to keep their high social status amongst their peers, will wind up in a job someday that they hate just to make others happy or to make themselves look good.

The Comparison Trap

Kids who constantly compare themselves to others and have diminishing self-worth because of it will continue that habit for life, which will lead to a lifetime taking anxiety pills and using other substances to fill the void.

Perfectionist Mentality

Kids who have the tendency to hyper-focus on the one thing they did wrong, as opposed to giving himself or herself a pat on the back for what they did *right,* will turn into miserable men and women who are perceived as negative and pessimistic by others.

Satisfaction is one of the keys to a happy life. Absent regular satisfaction, you will be devoid of a certain level of joy in your life that God wants you to experience. We want our kids to be satisfied, not complacent, but *satisfied* with their efforts when they give their best.

The FEAR of Rejection

"The fear of being judged or rejected can only be conquered by leaning INTO the fear when you feel it. You cannot go over, under, or around fear. You must go through it."

-- COACH ANDREW

This is a message to your athletes. The fear of rejection is real. It does not feel good. But it is necessary to go through it if you desire for your athletes to become confident earlier in life.

You must start living your truth. If you love God and believe in Him, yet the majority of your friend group does not, what would a confident person *do* in a situation where the topic of God came up? They would own it, never denying their faith. If you have *real* friends, they will likely not reject you for it. However, some will, and when they do, life will go on.

If you have a passion for painting, collecting antiques, fishing, or something that is unique to you, you need to own that. Don't be afraid to show it.

I know some athletes who give less than their best effort sometimes because they do not want to be judged by their peers. "Oh boy, there goes Johnny again. Overachiever. He thinks he is better than everyone."

Those words *hurt*. And they cause so many people who have the potential to stay average. So many people, youth and adults, have the potential to be extraordinary, yet because of the fear of being judged, they shrink down to a size smaller than what they were created to be. The pain of rejection outweighs the gain of being great.

Give your best effort all the time *no matter what*. If someone hates you for it, forget them. Misery loves company. You will inspire a handful to work harder while the one or two bad apples will try to pull everyone else down.

If you are compassionate to your core and find yourself getting emotional and caring about certain groups of people who are in need of help, embrace it. Sacrifice your private hitting lessons for one night per week of service at your local food kitchen or retirement home.

If you are an outgoing, happy-go-lucky, excited person, do not suppress that just because you have some friends who are Eeyores. I see this happen all the time and it kills me. You've got to be the thermostat, not the thermometer.

We have a kid that comes into our gym that smiles and gives high fives when it is raining outside.

You might be thinking, "OK?"

That is uncommon! *Most* people are affected by their conditions and environment. Most people, and particularly teens, are *thermometers.*

The Thermostat and the Thermometer

This is something all coaches or parents can teach their kids.

A thermometer's purpose is to *check the temperature.* It adjusts to the temperature of the room.

A thermostat, on the other hand, sets the temperature.

I believe our youth need to learn this analogy. They need to practice being confident being the thermostat. It is called *leading.* Thermometer living is *following.*

Think about it. Imagine if your son, your daughter, or your players decided that from this day forward they would be the thermostat. They made a firm decision that regardless of the weather, regardless of their friend's decisions or their friend's attitudes, regardless of their teacher's cutting remarks, that they would not be affected. They would commit to remaining positive, optimistic, and excited for the day. *Man!* What a world we would have.

This is *possible*. Everything rises and falls on *leadership*. Every person rises up or shrinks down based on their leaders. Love-powered leadership is the solution to building kids up. Could you imagine if your boss at work embraced some of the concepts in this book?

Some people *will* reject you for being a thermostat. After all, there are not many good leaders in any given classroom or sports field. If you begin to embrace your uniqueness, people *will* think you are weird and will say or do some hurtful things towards you. Whatever. Keep being you.

I once learned that suppression leads to depression. Suppressing your passions, your desires, and your true self in order to appease other people and conform to the social norm is a recipe for a sad, depressing existence.

Misery loves company, and people who spend every day trying to be someone they are not *are absolutely miserable.* When you hide your true self and try to be someone you are not, it causes more anxiety, stress, depression, and frustration than just about anything else. You were created to unleash the fullness of your passions, desires, and character.

Chapter 22

UNLOCKING LIMITLESS POTENTIAL

Amanda was a stellar lacrosse player who found herself battling a possible career-ending lower back injury. She was in college and was unable to play her freshman season due to the injury, which only seemed to be getting worse.

"Do I keep pushing what could be an immovable rock (also known as being stupid), or should I walk away from the game I love knowing that maybe, just maybe, my job here is done?" she asked herself.

As I will talk about more later in the book, quitting a sport is a decision that requires a ton of evidence gathering. Are you doing it for the right reasons? Did you seek a multitude of counsel? Did you wait long enough to ensure you are not making an emotional decision? These are all things to consider before an athlete should pull the trigger on quitting. However, in this case, I could sense Amanda had done her homework and was thinking deeper than, "What would be easiest for me?"

The point of me telling you this is that her parents, not thinking clearly, said the following words to her:

"You know what, Amanda? You always quit when things get tough. You quit your internship, you quit your relationship with David, now you are quitting this."

Stop right there. It is unlikely that Amanda heard *anything* that came out of their mouths next. Because she was hit at the heart level with the belief that says to herself, "I am the *type of person* who quits when things get difficult." We must remember that kids, even in college, take what we say to them to the *heart level* (belief). They are not good at discerning between an opinion and reality.

Three days after that conversation with her mom and dad, I thank the Lord that Amanda and I sat down to have a mindset session. I shared with her the same thing that I am about to show you – the Belief Cycle. If it were not for that meeting, Amanda may have spent years of her life with that belief ingrained in her heart and mind.

Imagine what her "results in life" would have been had we not worked to shift her perspective.

> Coach's note: Encourage your athletes at least once per week to share with you when a friend, coach, teacher, parent, or anyone of influence says something hurtful that makes them question their *character.* Words that influencers say to kids can have a lifelong impact on them if they are still *immature.*

Below is the one thing you need to grasp if you want to help your athletes *unlock their limitless potential.*

The Belief Cycle

The following continuum is one of the first lessons I teach during mindset coaching. It explains why trying to change your actions, habits, and results *before* addressing your core beliefs never works.

Beliefs (heart) → Thoughts (mind) → Feelings (flesh) → Actions → Habits → Results

A teacher named Judy decided to accept a position at a new middle school. Upon arriving, she was assigned by the administration to teach a classroom of about 20 children.

All semester long she taught them the most challenging material.

At the end of the semester the children were administered a school-wide exam. Her children absolutely crushed the test. Their scores ended up being the highest in the entire school.

The administration, shocked and confused, came to Judy the day after scores came out.

"How on earth did you get those students to perform so well! As you know, these were the least intelligent kids in the school. They scored lower on the test from last semester than anyone else. They've been in the directed classes for the past two years!"

"What do you mean?" asked Judy. "These kids are brilliant. You handed me their scores at the beginning of the semester, and they all scored incredibly high last year! Therefore I challenged them with the hardest material."

"Judy, those were NOT their test scores. They were their *locker numbers.*"

Let's break this down.

Beliefs → Thoughts → Feelings → Actions → Habits → Results

Beliefs. Judy believed their locker numbers were the student's test scores. Therefore, she believed they scored higher than they actually did.

Thoughts. Judy *thought* the kids were brilliant.

Feelings. Judy *felt like* they could handle the hardest material.

Actions. Day after day, week after week, month after month, Judy *gave* (action) them hard assignments, *taught* (action) them the hardest material, and *challenged* (action) them with hard projects, essays, and tests.

Habits. Obviously, this became a habit for Judy and for her students.

Results. Test scores increased and kids got smarter, but more importantly, the kids began to *believe* they were smart. *Their* thoughts about themselves had changed.

Because Judy's belief cycle about them changed, their belief cycle about themselves had changed. How cool is this, to know that you have the power to change the hearts and minds of your student-athletes?

What your athletes are good at today frankly does not matter and they need to know that. Where they are today simply is unimportant.

Their athletic performance, their social circle, their confidence, their time management skills, their attitude, and their communication skills *today* do not determine their results and future skill sets in those arenas.

However, their beliefs about *who they are* do matter. No belief change, no change. Period.

Take a student-athlete, Suzy, for example. If Suzy believes that she is only liked, valued, and accepted if she scores goals, earns 1st team all-conference, and earns straight As, then she will build the *habit* of perfectionism and she will do whatever it takes to gain that acceptance. Ultimately her results will be burnout, anxiety, and massive stress.

Deep down, if Johnny *believes* they he is a D3 caliber athlete, it does not matter if you and everyone else knows that D3 is below his potential and that D1 is possible. His *results* will be congruent with his *beliefs*. He will think like a D3 caliber athlete, act like one in his training, and end up at D3 school. Where he ends up is not the point – where he *could have ended up* had a coach helped him change his beliefs about himself is.

If your athletes believe that their voices will not be heard and that you, the coach, do not value their opinion, they will build the *habit* of keeping quiet and not having difficult conversations with you. This will lead to their personal *results* never changing, their circumstances never improving, and ultimately, it will wreck your team's culture and create one of fear and an "I'm just here to get mine" mentality.

Your athletes' skills, abilities, and results can all be changed if you can simply help them change what they *believe* about themselves *first*. I say "simply" because once you have the knowledge about how to do mindset training, and then you commit to allocating time, both in group settings as well as one-on-one with the athlete, it really isn't that hard to change the story your athlete is telling himself or herself. Once we do it with one, we can do it with *many*. Then the entire team wins.

What a powerful, encouraging thought for you and I. Change beliefs, change results, change lives.

A mentor of mine once told me, "*Never let your past experiences or your current circumstances limit your vision for the future.*" Now *that* is a powerful and encouraging thought for me, for you, and for every kid you'll ever work with. I often deliver that quote with massive effect to the athletes I work with.

One of the best things I have ever done for myself or for the student-athletes I worked with is to take them through introspective writing exercises like the ones I will give you in the future chapters of this book. Introspection leads to self-awareness, and self-awareness leads to self-improvement. Journaling is a lost art, but one that mindset coaching will force you to resurrect.

Chapter 24

THE PERSONAL POWER OF WRITTEN INTROSPECTION

"If you want to get the truth, have them write it down first."
-- ANONYMOUS

Kids have lost the ability to think, reason, comprehend, and weigh evidence. When it comes to sharing their thoughts and feelings, the current generation is worse than any previous generation in history. They are so deep into their Insta-feed that they are losing two powerful skills sets: self-awareness and vulnerable communication. They do not even know what they do not know. Despite hours of homework, kids are not really training their *minds*.

This is really not just a generational thing; it is a people thing. We, as adults, are similar in some ways. Many parents are completely unaware of how they have conformed to societal pressures and standards for their children. If they stepped out from the trenches long enough to get above it, they would witness the following common conformity trap in their own life: "If that parent is doing it and that kid is doing it, I need to and my child needs to do it as well."

The problem is that the *thought* of all of this isn't even occurring. Some parents are skipping the *thinking and reasoning* part and just doing stuff without considering the repercussions.

The perfect example is club sports that intrude on your finances and values. Parent #2 signs their kid up for a club sport because they heard Parent #1 signed their son up for it. Then Parent #2 complains about how expensive it is and how they can't get to church or do a real vacation now. Parent #1 may be financially secure and value tournaments over church or real family vacations, whereas Parent #2 does not. The problem? Parent #2 conformed without using their thinking and reasoning skills. That habit then gets passed down to their kids, and the crazy cycle continues.

Imagine if once a week, you had to write down the answer to the following questions:

What decisions was I tempted to make this week just because another parent was doing it?

What are my values? What are the things that matter MOST to me and my kids?

What are my ABSOLUTE NOs right now, the things that we as a family are not going to participate in, say yes to, or conform to?

Introspective writing exercises will transform your life. They will transform your athlete's too. Take the time to craft questions, or use the ones we give you, and have your student-athletes answer them. Because what happens next is golden.

Openness and Honesty

In Part 4 we give you numerous writing exercises to do with your athlete(s). When you do these, the coolest thing happens. They are open and honest.

We had a kid come into PFP who was struggling with body image issues and a potential eating disorder. His mother shared this with us over the phone about 30 minutes prior to their evaluation. During the evaluation, we first took the athlete through a self-guided questionnaire where they self-identify with different statements. Here is how it looked *before* his mother called.

The Confident, Successful Athlete: Questionnaire

Highlight or check off the following statements that are true, even a little bit

- On a scale of 1-10, 10 being the most motivated and committed to becoming the best athlete I can be, I am a _____
- I don't feel like I work on the mental game of sports enough
- My habits as a student are not the best, I want to get better
- I want to learn how to deal with difficult coaches better so that they do not negatively impact my confidence
- My communication is not the best. I don't communicate my thoughts and feelings as well as I should
- I believe improving my communication would help myself, my team, and my coaches
- I would like to have a mentor, a coach who cares about my success and holds me accountable
- I feel like my coaches don't really try to understand me, my goals, my fears, etc.
- I sometimes focus on things I can't control
- I focus more on the things I did not do well than the things I did
- I want to improve my confidence and self-belief
- I sometimes compare myself and my performance to others
- I sometimes doubt myself in GAMES, SCHOOL, and/or SOCIAL situations If I am honest, sometimes I try to be someone I'm not
- I play *down* to my competition sometimes
- My parents put a lot of pressure on me to play well and it's hard to communicate with them about it
- The fear of disappointing my parents, coaches, or teammates sometimes impacts my performance negatively
- I think my mindset is what is holding me back from my full potential
- I sometimes blame others for my attitude or results
- I sometimes make excuses instead of taking ownership and deciding to focus on what I can control
- When I mess up or make an error, it takes a while for me to come back from it
- I don't *always* do my BEST effort in school or sports
- I get nervous before competition and it affects my game
- I want to learn how to be a better leader but I don't have much experience and I don't know how to be a good one
- I want to learn how to get out of my own head and be "in the zone" more often during games
- I perform better in practice than I do in games
- I am not great under pressure
- I can let my emotions and frustrations get the best of me
- I wait until the last minute to do things
- I often wonder, "Who am I? Do I even matter?"
- I want to play sports in college
- I want to play professional sports

After we received that phone call from his mom, we added these statements in:

The Confident, Successful Athlete: Questionnaire

Highlight or check off the following statements that are true, even a little bit

- On a scale of 1-10, 10 being the most motivated and committed to becoming the best athlete I can be, I am a _____
- I don't feel like I work on the mental game of sports enough
- My habits as a student are not the best, I want to get better
- I want to learn how to deal with difficult coaches better so that they do not negatively impact my confidence
- My communication is not the best. I don't communicate my thoughts and feelings as well as I should
- I believe improving my communication would help myself, my team, and my coaches
- I would like to have a mentor, a coach who cares about my success and holds me accountable
- I feel like my coaches don't really try to understand me, my goals, my fears, etc.
- I sometimes focus on things I can't control
- I focus more on the things I did not do well than the things I did
- I want to improve my confidence and self-belief
- I sometimes compare myself and my performance to others
- I sometimes doubt myself in GAMES, SCHOOL, and/or SOCIAL situations If I am honest, sometimes I try to be someone I'm not
- I play *down* to my competition sometimes
- My parents put a lot of pressure on me to play well and it's hard to communicate with them about it
- The fear of disappointing my parents, coaches, or teammates sometimes impacts my performance negatively
- I think my mindset is what is holding me back from my full potential
- I sometimes blame others for my attitude or results
- I sometimes make excuses instead of taking ownership and deciding to focus on what I can control
- When I mess up or make an error, it takes a while for me to come back from it
- **I struggle with my eating. I do not eat enough.**
- **I believe I need to eat healthier**
- **I believe I need to drink more water**
- **I struggle with body image. I do not like the way I look**
- I don't *always* do my BEST effort in school or sports
- I get nervous before competition and it affects my game
- I want to learn how to be a better leader but I don't have much experience and I don't know how to be a good one
- I want to learn how to get out of my own head and be "in the zone" more often during games
- I perform better in practice than I do in games
- I am not great under pressure
- I can let my emotions and frustrations get the best of me
- I wait until the last minute to do things
- I often wonder, "Who am I? Do I even matter?"
- I want to play sports in college
- I want to play professional sports

You have to try this. What happens is this: we give the athlete the computer and tell them to "highlight and bold" the statements that resonate with them, the ones that apply to them.

Could you imagine if we just asked them the questions in yes or no format?

"Do you struggle with your eating?"

"No."

People, kids especially, feel attacked and get defensive when asked a question that reveals their flaws or insecurities. However, when they just have to "highlight and bold" statements that apply to them *even a little bit*, it is easier.

A great idea would be to create a self-evaluation form for your team, and then have them share with one another the things that are holding them back. We have done this with teams before and it is a moving and powerful experience. Vulnerability builds bridges of trust, connection, and understanding between people. It makes them feel less like they are alone on the journey. Kids already think that they are the "only ones" that struggle with certain things. When they hear their peers share out loud *their* struggles, they realize that none of their challenges are actually unique.

Assess *then* Correct

I remember one day an athlete came into our gym to work out and she seemed *off*. This girl was a rock star, high-level Division 1 commit for lacrosse. She *always* brought it. But today, she was moody. She had an attitude. I became offended when she refused to do chin-ups. I looked at her confused and said, "Ok, I guess we aren't getting better today. Go stretch, you can be done."

As she was foam rolling, I felt a nudge to go talk to her one last time. She was in tears. "My dad is in the hospital. He has a high risk of heart attack because he is overweight. And to make matters worse, my boyfriend broke up with me today."

If her body language and mood during the workout would have been sadness opposed to an angry, bad attitude, would *my* response have been different? It was a lesson learned for me as a coach: *seek first to understand, then to be understood.* People can and do respond to similar things with different emotions.

How often do we respond and react out of frustration or anger when *we* don't get what *we* want from our players? Then to take it one step further, why do *we* have the tendency to place unrealistic expectations on our athletes? What do we believe in our hearts that causes us to place these expectations on them?

Imagine if each day before practice, you gave each athlete a piece of paper to write on. You prompted them with the question, "What things are going on in my *personal* life today that could affect my on-field performance? How are those things making me feel?"

If you had your athletes write those things down for three minutes, then subsequently had a captain lead stretches while you and your coaches went through the responses, would it change the way you acted toward some athletes during the practice? Could it save you the regrets of anger and frustration towards a kid who just found out their parents were getting a divorce?

I have learned that the *reason* a kid is not talking or behaving the way you *want* them to is irrelevant. All that matters is that kid has something going on inside, and he wants someone who cares to take the time to listen and understand him – because his teenage male friends certainly are not doing that for him. He likely isn't sharing it with his parents. But the one person in his life who has the power to get through to him, his coach, is too busy thinking about the skills, drills, techniques, and tactics that he needs his players to execute so they can *win the game.*

While you may *win the game,* coach, you have lost the championship, which is helping young men and women to become leaders someday who care more about *people* than they do about *things.*

Don't major in minor things. Spend time planning out some writing exercises for your kids before or after practice. Include introspective, thought-provoking, clarity-providing questions that give them a chance to verbally or nonverbally *get things out of their heads.* Questions that make that young men or women really understand why they feel the way they do, think the way they do, and act the way they do.

Remember, when we do not let things out, we act them out.

Writing creates clarity, and clarity precedes progress.

A Challenge for You

I am not an expert coach or a guru by any stretch of the imagination. The more I learn about coaching, I am reminded of how much I don't know about coaching, and how much more I can grow. Something funny I heard recently is, "The difference between smart people and dumb people is that *smart people actually know how dumb they are,* whereas dumb people have no idea how dumb they are and therefore think they are smart!"

I know for a fact there are coaches who will read this book who are far better and more experienced coaches than I am. When I listen to the greats like John Wooden, Mike Krzyzewski, and Tony Dungy speak about coaching and developing young men and women into exceptional people, I am reminded of how much I still do not know.

However, I do know this:

Experience x Massive Action + A Burning Passion to see my athletes succeed as people = me becoming a greater coach of influence someday.

I know I have discovered a unique message that God wants me to share with the sports world and that I have a responsibility to share it through writing. I started paying attention to people's compliments a couple of years ago. I used to think humility was ignoring compliments, not letting them go to my head. What I realized was that not only should I graciously accept compliments, *but that consistent compliments leave clues about who you are and what you were designed to do more of.*

Young coaches, you must get this. Stop beating your head against a brick wall trying to work on your weaknesses and then passing that bad habit onto your athletes.

What happened was that I kept receiving great feedback about my blogs and articles. Parents and coaches would thank me for speaking up about a certain topic that was being ignored. It dawned on me toward the end of 2018 that I needed to stop worrying about making videos to spread my message, and instead I needed to amplify my strengths and *write more!* If writing is a gift God has given me, I should probably own it and use it.

And if *you* are a coach who enjoys writing and has a message to share, this is my one-time encouragement to you: *write*. Start writing. You do not need to have it all figured out. Just start. Don't be afraid of what others will think. Remember what Aristotle said, "To avoid criticism, say nothing, do nothing, be nothing."

Chapter 24

BAD QUESTIONS → BAD ANSWERS → REALLY BAD DECISIONS

As we have already mentioned, there *are* proven solutions out there that will help set your athletes up for a life of confidence, success, and leadership. But it starts with asking the right questions. For a long time, I asked the question, "How do I create the fastest, strongest, best performing athlete?"

Because that was my beginning question, my modalities and methods reflected it. I believe coaches are asking the wrong question. The question should not be, "How do I build a better athlete?"

The question should be, "How do I build a better *person*?"

My *personal* legacy question is, "How do I develop him or her into a more *confident, successful, servant-leader on and off the field?"* These are three things I think are at the top of the necessity list for youth today. Since that is now my starting question, my methods and modalities have changed dramatically. What I focus on, what I recognize, what I reward, what I teach, *and* what I reprimand is completely different than it used to be.

Friday Night Lights

I'm troubled by the reality that an athlete can become the best *on the field* with the help and guidance of a coach, yet that same athlete could end up broke, abusive, depressed, unsuccessful, lacking purpose, angry, bitter, and discontent with his or her life from age 22 to 85. Or worse, they could become a person who is stuck, complacent, and settling for a life that has no energy, drive, love, or meaning.

It's like the movie *Friday Night Lights*. Charles Billingsley, the father of the Permian backup running back Don Billingsley, was a former state champion. Charles and his team won states decades prior to his son being on the team.

When Charles and his football team won, I can assure you that he felt like he was on top of the world. Fast forward two decades, and Charles was a drunk, miserable, unsuccessful shadow of a man who was living vicariously through his son. He physically beat his son on numerous occasions for not being the star player that he wanted him to be.

Why do I say all this? I do not believe *you* are that coach. However, something we cannot afford to forget any longer is that if we help these young men and women to be the best on the *field* but fail to do our *best* at helping them be the best they can be in *life after sports,* we have failed.

I'll repeat again: by the standards of a love-powered, life-transforming coach, you will be a failure if you do not affect change in your athletes' *beliefs about who they are, the way they think, and ultimately their future decision making and the results that will follow.* We are not their saviors and we cannot control our athletes like robots, but leadership *is* influence. If you are not influencing their decisions, attitudes, and actions *off* the field, you have to face the brutal facts of reality. You are not succeeding, and it is likely because you have room to grow in your leadership and influence, as do I. If you are with me still, it means you and I are aligned in our values as coaches and we both have an ache in our hearts to build better *people,* not just temporary "winners."

I want you to imagine every athlete you work with right now, but 20 years older. If they are 16 years old, I want you to vividly imagine them at age 36. There are also apps for this kind of stuff now if you want to take it a step further and literally see what they might look like at age 36. What kind of father, mother, friend, professional, or volunteer would you like to see them become?

I want to remind you once again that you have the power to influence *who* your athlete becomes, not just what they do. You have the power to choose what you spend your two hours at practice teaching. You have the power to sit down one on one with a young man or woman and mentor them. You have the power to bring in guest speakers to talk with your team about life. You also have the power to share *your story* – the mistakes, struggles, and heartaches you endured growing up.

What gets prioritized by you gets valued by your players. If you place learning the playbook for a 10th time over playing a 10-minute Ted Talk that connects with their hearts and leads to a breakthrough, then prepare for the results to reflect that.

Step one is asking the right question. What will *your* questions be?

Here are some examples:

"What do I need to do as a coach to help my players *want to* play sports long after they *have to?"*

"Who do I need to be as a leader in order for my players to become leaders of integrity, consistency, and character?"

"How do I develop confident, successful, servant-leaders on and off the field? As a coach, how do I need to think and act? What do I need to do differently? What do I need to stop doing or start doing? What mental, emotional, or spiritual growth exercises do I need to do with my athletes?"

"How do I get Jamie to be confident in who she *is,* rather than her confidence being depending on what she *does?"*

"How do I get my coaching staff on board with me to completely change our approach and values that we have for our team?"

If you have trouble connecting answers to those questions, it means one thing. You need a mentor, a coach, someone who will help you find those answers. I can help and so can many others. If my style resonates with you, email me at andrew@pfpfit.com and I will do my best to serve you.

Chapter 25

SELF-WORTH: THE FOUNDATION OF CONFIDENCE

Jamie's Story

In November of 2018, a young girl came to us to train for her sport. I got the sense early on it wasn't what *she wanted*. However, she proceeded to tell us that she wanted to get stronger and improve her hand-eye coordination. Here's why:

Jamie's Goals (Jamie's Parent's Goals for Her)

1. **Get stronger:** her coach labeled her "the feather" because of how weak she was and how she would get knocked over so many times on the lacrosse field.

2. **Improve hand-eye coordination:** her dad paid her $2 every time she intercepted a pass on the lacrosse field. She wasn't really *motivated* to improve hand eye coordination, but as she told me, "I feel like I need to start intercepting more passes so that he is proud of me."

This highlights a major problem in youth sports today: **Jamie's self-esteem was diminished because of a *game*.**

Lacrosse is a game. Sports? Yep, they are games too. For .003% of the population, they *are* a job. However for the other 99.997%, it is a game. We cannot forget this, and neither can our athletes. This perspective alone is why an athlete will come to us feeling stressed, pressured, and insecure about their performance, and 30 minutes later they feel better. We remind them what ranks highest in their life.

Do I believe in giving a participation trophy to the kid who has a bad attitude and doesn't try?

No, but let's not forget who else besides that kid has shaped his or her *mindset*. There are other people responsible and accountable. That kid needs a positive sports experience to grow mentally. He needs love-powered coaches and teammates to have a shot at a great life. That kid has to have an enjoyable, uplifting, empowering experience with sports. It is non-negotiable.

That young man or woman should *never* be judged or made to feel inferior because he/she hasn't developed physical strength or speed. It is a *game!* One of my personal missions is to see to it that someday, no child's self-esteem would be diminished because of their athleticism, classroom performance, looks, or popularity.

You know what I told Jamie?

I told her that if she *wanted* to, it would be pretty simple to improve her strength and hand-eye coordination. Twelve weeks of strength training with an additional day or two of specific coordination drills with a coach would do it.

But why? To get the coach's approval of her? That coach would likely just find another area of her game to criticize and stick a label on her until she improved on that one too. I'm including this in the book not because *you* are that kind of coach, but because understanding what some athletes have had to deal with is important. Some coaches are really, really awful.

Understanding *why* an athlete is the way they are is a critical component to having a bigger influence in their life. We all crave to be understood.

"Coach gets me."

This is something every coach should long to be said about him or her.

I told her, "*I ONLY want you to workout at PFP if YOU want to. If you want to get stronger for YOU, do it. If you want to improve your skills for YOU, do it. But just remember, never let someone's opinion of you become your reality. And NEVER let your performance on the lacrosse field go to your head or your heart. Who you are on the inside plus the way you react and respond is 100 times more important than your physical strength and hand-eye coordination.*"

This is what I believe. We back it with how we reward, recognize, and correct our athletes.

Results are a by-product

We have parents that come to our business everyday looking for *results* – speed, agility, power, strength, and flexibility. And we deliver that.

But it is not our *why*. It is not our mission.

If you focus on developing the *root* of an apple tree, and the *fruit* will come. Focus on character, leadership, empowerment, self-belief, effort, and resiliency. Guess what happens?

As of August 2019, 71 of our student-athletes have either graduated from, are currently attending, or are currently committed to play college sports. The best part is, they are *all* of the same mindset now that sports are part of their life: they are not *who they are*. They are all becoming leaders in college, not followers. They are becoming "mature." We created a two-part definition of maturity and shared it with our college athletes in 2019. It goes along with the self-esteem talk, and goes something like this:

The Worst Definition of Self-Worth Ever

My Self Worth = My Personal Performance + The Opinions of other People

That is the definition for 99% of students in high school and middle school. This is a recipe for disaster, and here's why.

1. My Personal Performance

Even professional athletes know that they are not going to play great all the time. This realistic expectation of mistakes and failure helps guard them from feeling worthless during slumps or temporary defeats. We have an athlete we work with who has this definition on the back of her door now to remind her of why she *used to* feel worthless.

2. The Opinions of Other People

We cannot trust them. Why?

Because mom's opinion of my performance is that I played really well tonight based on my hustle, my defense, and the way I carried myself when the team was playing poorly. However, my dad clearly said (non-verbally, with his body language and lack of interest in talking to me after the game) that he thought I stunk it up. I did not score any goals and missed an open shot with two minutes left in the game.

If you let the opinions of people impact your self-esteem, your self-esteem will be the never-ending roller coaster that we have discussed throughout this book.

More confident men and women are built out of their understanding of unshakeable self-confidence.

We are all fickle. Let's face it. Our opinions about our athletes should never impact the way they feel about themselves. If they do, it is because that person was not equipped with the discernment between truth versus opinion. It is for this reason that I try to only let God's opinion of me matter.

I recommend that you take a major step of courage right now and teach your kids that even *your* opinion of their performance should not affect the way they feel about themselves. Does this make sense?

Of course your athletes would be wise to take your *advice* and work on the things you are encouraging them to work on. Train hard, train smart, and get better at every aspect of your sport, school, and life. I'm all about it. But again, self-esteem should never, ever, ever, *ever* decrease due to athletic or academic abilities.

If your athletes base their self-esteem on the wrong things now, they will continue to do it with their future professors, future bosses, future spouses, future friends. If they let *your* opinion of them diminish their self-esteem and belief in themselves, they will do it for others too. That is not what love-powered coaches are building here. We are building something far better. Leaders who know who they are and leverage their realistic view of their worth for the benefit of others.

Chapter 26

BECOMING UNSHAKEABLE(ISH)

*"Storm preparation is the key to surviving and thriving
during the storms of life."*
-- Anonymous

A big part of Mindset Performance Coaching is teaching students the discipline of planning and preparing for storms ahead. If you want to build up young men and women who may get knocked down but are strong enough to avoid getting knocked out, this is a mindset coaching lesson you will want to administer.

How often do you hear about one of your students going through adversity, big or small, and completely losing their cool?

A small example is traffic. We all hate when we are driving to a destination and forget to turn the GPS on. We run into a major crash on the freeway and are stuck in an extra hour of traffic that we *could have avoided* had we properly planned and mapped out the course in advance. That is what storm preparation is all about.

Have you ever thought about why some ships are able to survive major storms at sea, while others are not?

I had not until my dad passed away. There are lessons we can all learn from the way a ship plans and prepares to weather to scariest of storms. Here they are:

How the best crewmen prepare for storms:

1. They get the weather report.

To steer clear of hurricanes, mariners need good weather information.

This parallels to life's "storms." We all know that sickness, sorrow, pain, and death are going to happen. These are the conditions in life that are unavoidable.

So I think we should all be continuously running a "report" about which life storms may be in the near future. We should also prepare for the unexpected ones that may arise.

By doing so, we can "map out" our course of action.

Months ago I asked the questions, *"How would I act if my dad does pass away soon?"*

"What kind of person would I want to be in that moment? How would I want to show up for my family?"

It does not change the pain or sadness I am feeling right now. But it does make a difference.

2. The Ballast

I had no clue what this word meant, but apparently the most dangerous ship in a hurricane is an empty one. That's because the weight of cargo helps stabilize the ship against the waves.

"What will anchor me down when my dad does pass away?" I thought.

"What routines do I have that will help me?"

For me, I knew the answers:

- My morning power hour with God: Bible, devotional, journal, meditate
- Prayer with Daniela everyday
- Constant connection with my sisters and mom
- Working out every day, even if just stretching. Getting my body moving will be essential to my healing
- Eating well
- Keeping TV and screen time to a minimum so I can get quality sleep

Basically, I wanted to continue doing all the things that normally make me happy and feel good, amplifying a few of them as well.

These are the things that *ground me* in my life. And when a storm hits, I will avoid the temptation to run away from all of those good things.

3. They have ports to run to.

There are places along the route that the ship can head to for shelter if they see a storm coming. Great mariners look for these in advance.

The parallel to life here is, "Who will I talk with on a daily basis? A therapist? A friend? A pastor?"

I know and "preach" often that having someone to talk to is key to healing. So for me, it is my pastor, my best friend, and my wife.

I scheduled time each week to share my truest heart and talk through some of the scary things that happened with my dad over the past two weeks.

We all need "ports" to run to for help.

4. The crew knows which waters to avoid and which ones to go toward.

The crew has already thought about the storms. They have already planned out in their mind how they will react, which waters to head toward, and which to avoid.

This wraps it all up. I decided in advance I would *avoid* the shark infested waters of:

- Drug and alcohol consumption
- Binge watching TV and anything else that would distract my mind and take it off of the pain of losing my dad
- Eating "feel-good foods" (that only make you feel good when they are in contact with your taste buds, then make you feel awful)
- Shutting people out

And instead, I would run towards the waters that I have mentioned throughout this entire article:

- God
- My church family
- My immediate family
- My relatives
- My PFP family
- Great books
- My purpose in life
- Continuing the work my dad left for me

- Honoring him with the way I treat people and care for my family

So many beautiful waters to run toward.

With all that said, I shared with our student-athletes that it is *still hard*. "I've never had to grieve before, so I am learning a lot during this process," I told them.

I shared with them that I knew I would not be perfect during this storm and would not pretend to be. However, I do believe we can all learn from the best ships. I believe there are *better ways* to handle storms.

Our mission during the week we shared this message was for hundreds of student-athletes to be positively impacted by this message. Our hope was to use *my pain for their gain*. That is what God does, He flips the script. The Devil tries to rock the boat, and sometimes succeeds, but God always provides a way to use bad for someone else's good.

Do you want to be the coach that helps your athletes become more equipped to handle the future storms in their life with grace, poise, and integrity? If so, have them write down the answers to the following questions.

Who in your life will you turn to during storms? Who gives you the best advice, love, and support?

What kind of person do you want to be during a storm? How would the best version of you react if a serious storm happens?

As I have mentioned, it is important to always share your personal story and your personal answers to any introspective "mindset question" you ask your kids to answer.

I shared my storm about my dad with hundreds of athletes. I shared that article with thousands of people. I also shared with them where I *failed* to be the person I truly wanted to be in the time of a storm, but how I would do my best to never again let that happen.

This is a big one. Do not let this lesson pass through your mind without giving it to your student-athletes. Someone's life may be hanging in the balance. Knowing how to deal with major adversity in life the right way is a learned behavior, and they may not have a good example right now. Teach them about surviving and thriving in storms *before* the storm pops up.

You don't want to be the pessimistic guy or gal who always expects and plans for the worst. But wise people create *some* brain space for the if and when: 90% brain space for optimism, 10% for the realistic "what if."

Leaders go first. Do this exercise and share with your athletes!

Sarah Becomes Unshakeable(ish)

Sarah had just gotten home from her freshman year of college and she was crushed.

Here is what happened:

1st: A knee injury in the fall that set her back about eight weeks. *Not good* when you are on a scholarship and the coach *expects* you to produce results on the field. And despite being ready to go for spring season, coach had already written her off.

2nd: She was the victim of a form of some not-so-nice Senior bullying that took place.

3rd: She was called into the coach's office where he proceeded to tell her, "You are not as hard a worker as I thought you were. Maybe you are not cut out for college lacrosse."

I understand that this coach *thought* this was the way to motivate her, but it is not. That coach was not even close to truly understanding *how* Sarah was best motivated.

Those words penetrated her mind *and* her heart, and these were the results of all three things:

1. **Sarah was in tears** in my office three days after returning home for summer vacation.

2. **By the time freshman year was over, she had built the false belief** in her mind and heart that her scholarship was a result of pure *luck*, that she was *not* meant to be there (not a shocker, since the coach planted that seed of doubt).

3. **The injury was healed physically but stuck with her mentally.** She was running and cutting at 80% speed.

4. **The emotional pain** that came from the notion that she wasn't accepted or liked by the "leaders" was the breaking point that *almost* caused her to quit the game she loved playing for the past 13 years.

Long story short, after one hour in the office of us talking through this together, teaching her the Becoming Unshakeable framework, and having her do the introspective writing exercises that accompanied it, this is what she said:

"I'm ready. Can we go train? I want to get prepared for the fall season."

We do not believe in sugar coating things with the athletes we work with. We do believe that going through tough stuff can make them tougher.

But something amazing happens when you dive deeper into the *"why"* questions and seek to connect with their hearts.

"WHY is this particular kid so fragile? WHY does he/she have trouble making sense of their circumstances and seeing things through a more positive, optimistic lens?"

What happens is that you begin to realize that they are not yet wired for resilience, optimistic realism, or positive thinking. As you already know, 14-year-olds are *still kids*. Most 19-year-olds are still kids in the sense that their perspectives on life and life's challenges are still being shaped. Sarah really did need a coach or mentor at that particular point in time to *make sense of the situation for her.*

She needed a coach who was able to give her a different perspective. At the end of the day, I was not able to change anything that happened *to her*. I simply helped her realize it happened *for her* – that she could *choose* her response moving forward, and that it was actually her *response-ability*. Little by little, she began to see growth opportunities and ways to get better from that "horrible situation."

"Honor the struggle," as my mentor Brendon Burchard puts it. It becomes a way of life after you go through a few rounds in the ring with *life*. You start to realize that the punches make you stronger. That you learn how to dodge them, absorb them, learn from them. And when you get knocked down, you realize that the pain is temporary. You realize that even if you get knocked out, there is always a *next fight*.

Not sure about you, but for me, I *still* need that kind of mentoring and coaching in my life. How much more for a 19-year-old who may have not been equipped with the proper mindset tools growing up?

Do your athletes have the armor they need to proactively battle against the following things?

1. Injuries or major illnesses
2. Negative, unhelpful, hurtful words that come from coaches, peers, or influencers
3. Coaches decisions that do not align with their expectations or desires
4. Unforeseen setbacks
5. Friends' or teammates' negativity and drama
6. Family or friend crises

Do they continue moving forward in confidence?

I have found that so much of becoming *more* unshakeable lies in the *planning and preparation phase*. Taking deliberate time, focus, and attention to think about what happened, how did you respond, and how would the person you *want* to become respond in future situations.

As a response to Sarah's situation, we decided to create the "Becoming Unshakeable(ish) Masterclass." It is part of an online mindset course for student-athletes who want to develop that *unshakeable confidence*. We say "ish" because at the end of the day, we are all human. We will all be shaken on some level. You can visit www.andrewjsimpson.com to learn more about the course. But to start, simply talk through this exercise with your athletes. Go through the "Six Things That Shake Us" above and have them rate themselves on how *unshakeable* they currently are.

Chapter 27

BLINK AND SPORTS ARE GONE

Make Your Mess Your Message

So many kids struggle with humility, identity, and resiliency **through adversity** is because these two truths have not yet sunk in:

1. Your mess becomes your message.

2. You are **more** than an athlete.

Eight years ago, I started working with a lacrosse player named Lara. She went on to play at a major D1 school. In early 2018, she learned her career was going to be cut short. She was forced to medically retired due to a long-term injury that finally took its toll on her.

She was devastated, lost, confused and lacking clarity of purpose and direction. She had incredible, supportive parents, but she was still shaken up and in need of guidance.

Why?

Despite parents who told her otherwise, her identity *had* been tied up in sports for the previous 15 years of her life. For more than 75% of her lifetime, she had identified herself as an *athlete*. Can you blame her? It is tough to because of these three statements:

- Our value and sense of purpose comes from what gets rewarded and prioritized in our lives.

- Our identity and self-esteem come from the things for which we receive praise and recognition.

- We give full-ride college scholarships worth hundreds of thousands of dollars to kids who are good at a game. (This is a soap box moment, so bear with me.)

I applaud the student-athletes who recognize their gift of athleticism that God gave them and then choose to turn it into something more. However, there is *one crucial point* that needs to be addressed here if you want your son or daughter to avoid a common pitfall amongst young adults. The fact that our society values sports, even *college* sports, enough to give tens to hundreds of thousands of dollars to *one kid* makes those kids very financially lucky. I hate using the word "lucky" because they *are not lucky for becoming great at their sport.* I would never minimize the sacrifice and hard work that they put into their sport.

However – and this is a big however – they *did* hit the lottery in the sense that we as a society place a higher financial value on sports than just about anything else.

I believe all student-athletes need to be reminded of these two things:

- **BLINK and sports may be gone, just like they were for Lara.**

- **The prestige, money, fame, honor, and whatever else your child might receive from sports is only as beneficial as the extent to which they are willing to "give it away" and use that power to help others.**

If this message fails to slip into the mind and heart of your son or daughter, they may end up leading **empty, unfulfilling** lives, always chasing after the next carrot and wondering why they don't "feel happy."

So I sent Lara the following message. It is one I should have reminded her of long, long before.

"You know, I was thinking about you today and I came to a conclusion that maybe you have not considered. Your TRUE STRENGTHS are:

#1. Your crazy hard work ethic (passionate stubbornness at times :-))

#2. You innate ability to be a leader. You've never been afraid to step up and away from the crowd.

#3. Your infectious personality, the fact that people like to be around you, that you are a great conversationalist and aim to help other people.

For so long, you have used those things for sports. How awesome is it going to be when you figure out what the next "thing" is that you are supposed to use those gifts for? Pray. Ask God for guidance. He smiles when He sees you use your gifts to help others.

Maybe it's coaching? Idk, but all I do know is that you are a rock star of a person. You are far more than just an athlete. You have always amazed me.

Have a great weekend, keep inspiring others. :)"

Her response back:

"Thank you so much. Really needed that. Even though I couldn't play, I brought an entirely new attitude to practice today after reading that."

She is going to go on and be successful in whatever she does for the rest of her life, not because of what I said, but because she has a support group that is pouring into her right now, reaffirming to her that her value and identity have never been in sports alone. Her true strengths are what *allowed* her to be great at lacrosse.

An exercise that every love-powered coach will take their athletes through is this one: true strengths versus sports skills. It is as simple as sitting them down as a team, each with a pen and paper, writing down what their *true gifts, strengths, and talents are.*

Do all you can to become the best *you* can be, athlete. Use what you have been given for good. Just don't forget that you are more than an athlete. You have so much good to give the world.

Sports are simply a *vehicle* to use and develop your gifts, bring joy to your life, and help others.

Help Your Athletes Avoid Sports Superiority Syndrome

I worked with an athlete who as a freshman, received a full scholarship to play D1 soccer at one of the biggest soccer schools in the country. You know what that did for him?

Blew his head up to five times its original size.

Why? Because he forgot that soccer was just a game, that he was gifted with the ability to play a game.

The *only* reason this accomplishment caused him to get cocky and make him feel so good about himself was because our culture values sports so highly and pays professional athletes astronomical amounts of money.

Side note: Just like any other gift or talent, a gifted athlete can and should be proud of his or her ability. Humility is having a realistic view of one's importance. With that said, a humble athlete will recognize that being good at sports does not make him more important than anyone else. If they do not recognize it, it is a love-powered coach's responsibility to teach them this.

I had to talk to him.

"Steve", I said to him, "What gift have you been given?"

"Soccer," he said. "I am a great soccer player."

"Yeah, and you have also worked your tail off to develop that gift. I would consider you exceptional at the game of soccer, especially for your age. Would you agree?"

"Yes, I suppose you are right," he replied, trying hard to be as humble as possible in front of his coach.

"Good. Just make sure you do not forget that *your* gift of being great at soccer is no more valuable than one of your peer's gifts of being a great encourager. Or another kid who is a great teacher. Or a great listener, a great writer, a great dancer, a person who is great at working with kids with mental disabilities, or a person who is great at math or science. Never forget that being great at a game is no more valuable than anything or anyone else," I said to him.

He understood. But many do not hear those words.

Just because the majority of people idolize great athletes doesn't mean you need to. Just because the majority of people allow their gift of sports, good looks, or popularity to make them feel way too good about themselves doesn't mean you need to.

Why? Because those things will turn on you faster than you can blink.

I find it uncomfortably odd how many athletes, coaches, and parents operate day to day as if middle, high school, and club sports are not temporary, as if they are never going to end.

Despite us all knowing how short a window we have with sports and how temporary and empty the accomplishments really are, we still invest so heavily into the game.

I'm all about giving your best effort, but let's have a moment of transparency. Do you get more passionate and emotional about sports, which are temporary, than you do about your family's physical health, fitness, and well-being, which will be just as important in 50 years as it is today?

I recently picked up recreational basketball after not touching a ball for over a year. When you don't pick up a basketball for a year, you become really bad at basketball. It's like you're a child again trying to learn how to dribble, shoot, and pass. I found myself getting discouraged and literally feeling bad about myself after the first couple of games.

Then I realized, *duh!* Really, Andrew? You are allowing rec basketball to dictate your self-esteem. HA! What in the world are you valuing right now, the process of getting back in basketball shape? The fun of competing again and being on a team? Or my personal abilities and how good I was at passing, shooting, and dribbling?

Sounds ridiculous when you put it that way. It's a no-brainer. Having fun, getting back in shape, getting "good" again, competing, and playing on a team was way more important than how many points I scored. But just as quickly as I wrote these words, I forgot them and allowed what *other people said was important* to dictate what I felt was important at the time.

If athletes allow good plays, good games, good seasons, or good accomplishments to get them feeling too good about themselves, then they must prepare for the day(s) sports turn on them and leave them feeling worthless, depressed, and flat-out bad about themselves too.

My recommendation? Keep sports on the level of importance that they are supposed to be – below the most important things in life.

What are the most important things? You decide. And once you do, do not allow anything else such as sports or grades to ever allow you to get to high or too low on yourself.

Chapter 28

LEADING THROUGH CHAOS

I fear that most of our youth lack the ability to lead their lives confidently and courageous in the absence of peace and certainty. **Most people only have the structure to handle life when life is easy.**

The business you and I are in is one where we help others increase their capacity to perform *whether or not things are going their way.*

One of my values is to lead with integrity and positivity. Making this decision each morning makes me more likely to *remember it and be it* when things go wrong. Having clearly defined values is the best thing I ever did for myself and those I lead.

> *Note: Private hitting coaches and pitching coaches are AWESOME, if that is truly what your athlete needs most right now. Remember to always ask the question, what matters MOST right now? Am I investing the appropriate time, money, and energy into THAT thing? Is it a trade-off to something else more important?*

Core Values

Most of us have a *values discrepancy* in our coaching, parenting, and teaching.

These are the things we *say* matter most to us:

1. That our kids are mentally, emotionally, and physically ***healthy***
2. That our kids **enjoy** their sports, activities, and have fun
3. That they give their **best effort** in all they do
4. That they become young men and women of **character**, **great teammates**
5. That they learn valuable **life lessons** from school and sports such as teamwork, leadership, dealing with adversity, and overcoming fear

Yet we still shine the biggest spotlight on, give the most prestigious awards to, and pay the biggest bucks to those who have the best score, the most wins, and the best overall numerical results.

What gets recognized and rewarded gets repeated and prioritized.

Parents *say* that they don't care if their kid is the best, yet their verbal and non-verbal actions say otherwise after a game in which their child physically underperformed.

Coaches *say* that the scoreboard is not the entire story, yet they fail to lift the team up and congratulate them for small signs of progress, looking at *what isn't,* rather than shining a light on *what went well.*

Getting more intentional about creating and living your coaching values will help you overcome the temptations to get caught up in what *other parents or coaches* say is most important. Define what matters most to you, then let your *game-plan* flow from it.

We *say* that work-life balance matters. That God comes first. That quality time for the family is top priority. That schoolwork comes before play.

So why do I hear kids all the time telling me that they missed church for the entire 2017 year (exaggeration added) because their tournament schedule was out and college coaches were going to be there?

I think to myself. God wasn't there. He was waiting for you in church.

Note: I am human too. This is why I set up guardrails in my life and surround myself with people who keep me on track and remind me to live my values out daily.

I love helping kids with their stress, but why do we have to help SO MANY KIDS overcome their stress and anxiety? Is it really necessary for a kid to get home from practice at 10:30 p.m. three nights a week and then have to stay up until midnight doing their homework? It does not seem like the things coaches and parents are saying they value are actually being acted upon.

I literally had a conversation with a mother *about this book* last week. She was telling me how much she loved the concept. She told me that it drives her nuts that her husband is so focused on winning, elite performance, and his daughter being *the best*.

After that conversation, we discussed the benefits of her daughter doing some mindset coaching since she was struggling with stress, confidence, her identity, and her worth.

Get this: she told me that she *wished* she had time for it but that SHE had just signed her daughter up for a *third league!* Her daughter was getting home at 11:00 p.m. three nights a week and was doing her homework in the car.

She didn't say this, but I provided the commentary in my mind: "Sorry, no time. My daughter, who is 12 years old and struggling mentally, needs to go to see her club coach. It's all good, he has a core value. It's called 'get more money for my business at the expense of the long-term mental health and well-being of my athletes.'"

Now, if that coach was taking time during the practice to help his athletes work on time management, stress management, maintaining positive relationships and well-being, then fine! The athletes do not *need* to be in our doors. We do not *need* their money. God provides for our business, not the parents.

However, since I *know* that we deliver on the areas of development kids are craving and in need of the most, I obviously feel a responsibility to lead them into our doors. We back up our values with our *actions*. If we don't, we lose credibility and eventually lose business. Integrity and value-based business practices are the *only way* to have an organization that is built to last.

What we *say* matters most doesn't mean squat. What we *give* our attention, time, money, and energy to *shows* what we value as most important.

Chapter 29

TOUGH DECISIONS ARE LONG-TERM INVESTMENTS

Ready to hear a sad, head-scratching story?

In 2018, we hosted a live talk at our gym. The talk was titled, "Keeping Your Child Safe from Online Sexual Predators: Something Every Parent Needs to Hear."

A very influential person from the FBI who deals with this problem on a large scale was to be the speaker. We promoted it to thousands of parents. We chose a time that we knew parents could make. Because really, what parent wouldn't prioritize one hour to learn about how to keep their social media, internet addicted teenager safe from thousands of online sexual predators and pedophiles out there?

During this talk, the parents in attendance (myself included) learned that we truly did not know what we did not know. It was mind blowing to hear the sophistication of these predators, *where* they are targeting children, *how* they are targeting children, and *how many kids have already been victims* but are completely unaware of the fact that they are victims. Pictures and videos of thousands of teens are circulating the child pornography industry without that child having a clue! The teenager thought he was sending the naked picture or sexual video to another cute teenager of the opposite sex, when in reality, it was a 45-year-old pedophile with a made-up account!

We learned of the countless stories of teens who have harmed themselves or committed suicide because they finally learned that they *were* victims. Through acts like sextortion, the predators essentially blackmailed these children one after another to the point where the shame and guilt of the child grew so great that they could no longer take it!

So what is my point of sharing all of this? You are probably thinking to yourself, "I was not expecting this to be in a youth athlete development book."

The point is this: there were twelve parents and three teenagers in attendance for this talk.

Thousands of parents saw that we were hosting this talk. They knew what was on the line. They knew this was an opportunity for them to have a transformational, future altering moment with their teen.

Yet, their lack of attendance proved either that something else was *more* important or that they were in denial. *"This could never happen to my kid."* I assure you that the six lacrosse games that weekend were not more important than the sexual predator talk.

Coaches and parents, we have a values discrepancy. It is not good. Our values are the foundational base of who we are. If we can't get clear on *our* foundation, we cannot develop a confident, successful young man or woman who ends up living a values-driven life as well.

Every week I have to rewrite my values, pray, and meditate on them. I'm not ashamed to admit that I need this extreme focus and accountability in my life to stay on track and on mission. I ask myself weekly, "Are my actions aligning with who God wants me to be? Am I spending my time and energy on the things *He* wants me to spend my time and energy on?"

I have to do this values assessment *weekly* because I know how easy It is to fall victim to the temptation to spend my time and energy on what *others* say is most important.

If all I am thinking about are short-term pleasures and what feels good and right *now,* I will go to watch the football game instead of attending the sexual predator talk every time!

And this leads us to the most important exercise you will ever do as a coach or parent.

Chapter 30

MORE IMPORTANT THAN SUCCESS IS...

It was the fall of 2017, and everything around me seemed to be moving 10 times faster than I could handle. It was a scary time in my life. Our business was growing rapidly, which is far from bliss if you have ever led a scaling business. I was newly married. I was involved in my church youth group. And I was trying to build an online brand that would impact youth athletes all around the world.

On two separate occasions leading up to that conference, I had two "attacks" of some sort. I'm not sure if they were anxiety attacks, panic attacks, or near heart attacks. Whatever they were, I was extremely concerned for my health. My heart would be racing, vision blurred, feelings of extreme overwhelm and doom would come upon me many times in a given day.

I learned of a conference taking place in San Diego in October. It was called the "Perfect Life Retreat." Sounded like a pretty good title to me. A guy named Craig was hosting it. Reluctantly, I jumped on the opportunity and decided to take my wife, Daniela, with me. She was concerned about my health, and for good reason. I say *reluctantly* because the timing, in my mind, could not have been worse. But God gives us instincts for good reason, because *His* timing is always perfect. He gave me the nudge, and I bought the ticket.

The retreat was a defining moment in my life. On day one, we did an exercise called "Values and Vision." This is an exercise I have since taken hundreds of other people through because of the massive impact it had on *my* life.

I sat there for 30 minutes and pondered the question, "What matters *most* in my life?"

I started writing…

1. My relationship to God, strengthening it, and drawing closer to Him.

2. Being a servant leader; selflessly and humbly leading my wife, my family, my team members, and the kids I coach who look up to me.

3. Fulfilling my professional purpose in life; running *at and through* my fears every day so I can fulfill the assignments He has called me to.

4. My personal health and fitness; taking care of my mind and body through clean nutrition, consistent exercise, and quality sleep.

5. Mentoring; teaching others what I have learned to help them improve the quality of their lives; generously giving away my most precious commodity, my time.

Those were my top five values. Great, now what?

It was analysis time. Self-evaluation time. How are you doing, Andrew, really?

Based on what you *say* matters most to you, are you living a life that is *congruent* with your values?

I was living one of them. Consistently, through my actions, I was still putting God first. But that was it. The others? They took a backseat.

No wonder I was on the verge of a fallout. I was stressed beyond control, overwhelmed, constantly anxious, impatient, and frustrated most of the time.

What you value is displayed by what you give the *bulk* and the *best* of your time, money, energy, and attention to.

When your values and actions are misaligned, the results are predictable. You are never at ease. You never feel *great.* Notice I said the *best* of your time, money, energy, and attention. Giving your leftovers to something or someone only shows how *little* you actually value that person or thing.

My Personal Values Discrepancy

You see prior to that conference in October 2017, here were my two values *based on my actions:*

1) God. I was still waking up every morning spending time with Him, one hour of Bible study, prayer, and journaling with my wife. *I believe this is the ONLY reason I did not completely break during that time.*

2) Work. I was working 14 hours a day – 10 hours on PFP and four hours building this online business that would change the world.

Where did leading my wife, family, team, and clients fit into this? It didn't. I led by position, not passion and protection like good leader does. I led with my leftover energy. And a few of our team members that I mentor decided to *follow the leader*, charging forward with grit and hustle at the expense of their relationships and physical health. How dumb was I?

Where did mentoring fit into this? I scrambled at the end of each night to send some "encouraging" text messages to college students I mentored, to my sisters, and to my team. I gave them my leftovers.

Where did my physical health and fitness fit in? It really didn't. I was getting four hours of sleep per night, working out one or two days a week at best, and drinking a considerable amount of coffee.

"At least it was organic," I justified.

Where did my purpose fit into this? It *sounds* like it fit well. But I now know that whenever you have to sacrifice personal well-being and relationships, you have to wonder, "Does God *really* want me doing this right now?"

So I ask you: what are *your* values?

What types of things are most important to you? What do you value for your kids or the kids you work with? What have you been *saying* is important but *displaying* otherwise?

I am about to have you stop reading and start writing. Answer this question: what do I value *most* for the kids I parent, coach, or teach?

Write out your list and then compare it to the things you and/or your student-athlete are giving the *bulk and best* of their time, resources, energy, and attention to. Reading this book for example, is showing that you value the mental health of your kids. Why? Because you spent *money* on this, and you are taking *time* to read it.

The parents who say they value mental health for their kids and then actually invest time and money into mindset coaching for their kids are aligning their *values* with their *actions*. Because they value the mental development, leadership development, confidence, and long-term success of their child, they spend more time and money on that than they do hiring another hitting instructor or pitching coach.

In Part 4, I have given you the actual Values exercise we do with our coaches and athletes. But I am going to ask you to stop right now and begin the process of Value Clarification. What are they for you?

Chapter 31

STAND OUT TO BE OUTSTANDING

"If you continue doing things the way you have always done them, you will continue to experience the results you have always experienced."

-- UNKNOWN

Mindset training has been the greatest thing we have ever implemented for our student-athletes at PFP because it is *different*. It allows us to stand out and it inspires them to as well.

When asked what made him the best hockey player of all time, Wayne Gretzky said this: "Most guys skate to where the puck is. I skate to *where it is going."*

Have you taken the time to recognize where the puck is *going*, coach? We live in the age of anxiety, stress, burnout, injuries, comparison, and low confidence. Don't you think that you will be most successful and your players will be most successful if you start providing the correct solutions to the biggest problems?

Mindset coaching encapsulates the best of all things youth development. Anything that improves a kids ability to overcome fear, encourages them live more selflessly, helps them to prioritize their time based on values, improves their self-worth and confidence, inspires and equips them to be a leader, or helps them in any other way than simply to "get ahead, get rich, get popular, and get better at sports" can be considered *Mindset Coaching*.

Get in the game. What got you here won't get you there. You need a new strategy. If you want to leave an admirable legacy, it's time to move. Let's dive into the exact exercises that you are going to take your student-athletes through.

Summary of Part 3:
Training the Mind

- "Mindset coaching" can literally be anything that helps a kid grow in an area of their life *outside* of the physical: leadership, overcoming fear, doubt, worry, learning to overcome mistakes, learning how to get in the zone, becoming more confident by knowing who they are. Mindset coaching is the key that unlocks the *inside* of a kid so they can perform at peak potential on the *outside*.

- *Belief Cycle – You* must change the story deeply ingrained in your athletes' minds before you will ever change their results. This requires more mental and emotional exertion on your part, but love-powered coaches always give more.

- Self-esteem starts in the heart and goes to the mind. If a kid's worth is tied up in how well they perform, they *will* end up disappointed. Help your kids redefine what brings them a sense of meaning and worth in their life, and make sure sports performance is not on the list.

- Start with the right question. How do I build a better *athlete* versus how do I develop a better *person?* Begin with the end in mind.

- Writing creates clarity, and clarity precedes progress. If you want your athletes to open up about what is holding them back, their desires, and their frustrations, have them write it first.

- Align your values with your actions. Define what you want your mark to be as a coach, what matters most to you, then live it daily.

- Dare to be different. Keep doing the same thing, keep watching your players struggle with injury, fear, doubt, and low confidence. Extraordinary results require not just *extra effort* but doing things *out* of the ordinary.

- Novelty. Newness is something we all need if we want to be our best and keep motivation high. Try something new with your athletes: read a book, bring in a guest speaker, do writing exercises together and have them share out loud.

Part 4

PUTTING IT INTO PRACTICE

How many kids do you know who are their own worst enemy and cannot get out of their own way? Athlete or not, their fears, doubts, and worries cripple them and hold them back. They are stuck in their heads. Their physical game may be strong but they've never really worked on *mental preparedness,* and therefore they never play to their full potential *consistently.* How true is that for *most* people, not just athletes?

Mental preparedness has two subsets in Part 4: Game-Ready Mental Preparedness and Life-ready Mental Preparedness.

Game-ready includes practical lessons such as getting into the zone and out of your head during games. It includes lessons that help you teach your athletes to create their Mistake Ritual which will help them to quickly overcome errors and mental blocks during games so that they have bad *plays* rather than having an entire bad *game.*

The Game-Ready Mental Preparedness section includes a lesson that teaches the athlete how to find their optimal state of mind before games, finding the balance between having low energy and excitement and having massive anxiety and worry. Finding that perfect balance for each individual requires an understanding of what psychologists call the "U-Curve."

Life-ready is about mental preparation that allows one to have more confidence and resilience in all areas of life. Since we know that *compartmentalizing* does not work and that an athlete's ability to handle difficult relationships or overcome a traumatic life event *will* affect their athletic performance, it is all relevant to sports. This section includes things like how to survive and thrive during the storms in life, how to redefine your confidence and avoid the rollercoaster effect, and how to define your values and vision for your life to avoid comparison to others and *losing yourself.*

When you help a young man or woman get better in *life,* they will reward you and themselves with better performance in sports and school. It's just the way it works. I've even found this to be true in business leadership. When I help one of our team members with a personal struggle or I help them to achieve a desire or life goal, the natural response is to give more to the team and the cause. It is the law of reciprocity.

The challenge is that most coaches and parents are unaware of all of the exercises they can administer that will help their kids personally and athletically, the exercises they can do to strengthen confidence, connection, and likelihood of success. The other challenge is that most coaches nowadays are too busy to mentor. It is a troubling truth that most coaches are so consumed with the pursuit of greatness that they have forgotten that mentoring a young man or woman through the storms of life and the rocky terrain of middle school, high school, or even college is far more significant and meaningful than improving batting average or winning percentage.

Let's work together in this next section to learn the key lessons we need to prioritize in order to see our student-athletes become stronger *people.*

GAME-READY
MENTAL PREPAREDNESS

THE MISTAKE RITUAL

Your #1 tool to overcoming mistakes quickly

I learned this back in 2017. I have taught courses on it to hundreds of athletes one on one. Here are some of the results:

"Thank you for teaching me the mistake ritual yesterday, Coach Andrew. I hit a double today. Finally got out of the slump! I've been using what you taught me!"

"Another update, I've been using it and hit a double *and* a home run today!"

Another girl had been in a slump with softball for five games straight. We taught her the mistake ritual. The next day, literally, she was in the newspaper.

The headline read: "Alex explodes out of his slump. Drives in game-winning three-run triple in the last inning to give the team the victory."

College athletes from Division III up to Division I. High school athletes. Middle school. You name it. The mistake ritual is a golden tool every athlete needs in their toolbox. Game-ready mental preparation requires this tool because errors, mental blocks, mistakes, and distractions *will never cease to exist.* Here is how you teach it.

Step 1: Reset Word

This is a word you will help guide your athlete to choose for his or herself, something that triggers their mind to think about moving *past* the mistake or distraction, moving on, forgetting about it, and focusing on what is ahead. It is designed to help them have, as my mentor and friend Todd Durkin says, "Short-term memory loss."

"Forget about it."

Words like, "Onward, dominate, overcome, focus, relax, breathe, next play, move on, let it go, NEXT!" These words and more will work. The key is for it to be *their* word, not yours. There should not be a "team reset word." It really does need to be customized.

Step 2: Hand Signal

Thumbs up by your side. Wiggle your fingers. Clap your hands once (specificity is important). Pat your sides three times. Wipe the left side of your hair. Make a fist and then release it. Shake out the hands. Again, help the athletes pick their thing by giving them specific examples.

Step 3: DEEP BREATH!

We breathe 18,000-22,000 times per day. Breathing is vitality and relaxation. This breath happens simultaneously while the athlete is saying the word in their head *and* doing their hand signal all at the same time.

Make sure to go to www.andrewjsimpson.com/book-insider to download the actual exercise that you will hand to your athletes to fill out. Remember, writing down your own mistake ritual creates clarity and ownership.

If you are a parent, make sure to go easy on the "coaching." I would recommend "suggesting" this because you happened to come across it and believe it would help anyone, including you!

The mistake ritual is an absolute game changer. Imagine a team full of athletes who never dwells on the past, that never gets stuck in long-term slumps. *Belief* that the mistake ritual works *is important.* Share my examples, read this section of the book out loud to them, and then start gathering your own testimonials as you are blown away by the effectiveness of the mistake ritual.

THE U-CURVE

Understanding the State of Mind, Body, and Emotion You Must Get into in Order to Perform Your Best

Have you ever seen an athlete who bounces around before games, pumped up, energetic, and seems to be on loads of caffeine?

What about an athlete who sits quietly before games, not moving much, listening to music? An example of this kind of athlete is Michael Phelps.

Some athletes play best when they are hyped up before and during the games, whereas some athletes play best when they are more calm.

Which is better, being pumped up and energetic before and during the games or quiet, laid back, almost chill?

NEITHER! All that matters as an athlete is that you know what your sweet spot is and you aim to get there *consistently*.

The U-curve, as you see in the provided graphic, is finding your area of best performance.

So the question is: do you play best when you are super pumped up and excited, super chill and relaxed, or somewhere in between?

Teach your athletes this concept and make sure to download the other resources and videos on this topic by going to www.andrewjsimpson.com/book-insider.

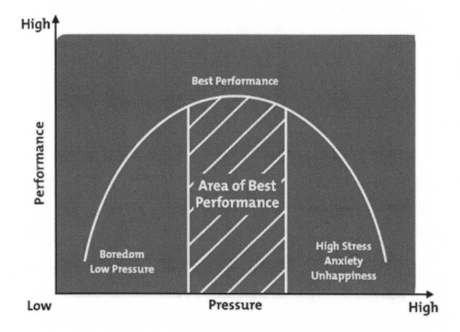

Lesson 3:

HOW THE BEST OPERATE "BETWEEN POINTS"

Here is an excerpt from the book *The Power of Full Engagement* by performance psychologist Jim Loehr:

*"To live like a sprinter is to break life down into a series of manageable intervals consistent with our own physiological needs and with the periodic rhythms of nature. This insight first crystallized for Jim when he was working with world-class tennis players. As a performance psychologist, his goal was to understand the factors that set apart the greatest competitors in the world from the rest of the pack. Jim spent hundreds of hours watching top players and studying tapes of their matches. To his growing frustration, he could detect almost no significant differences in their competitive habits **during** points. It was only when he began to notice what they did BETWEEN points that he suddenly saw a difference. While most of them were not aware of it, the best players had each built almost exactly the same set of routines between points. These included the way they walked back to the baseline after a point; how they held their heads and shoulders; where they focused their eyes; the pattern of their breathing; and even the way they talked to themselves."*

What made the best athletes different from the rest of the pack?

1. The way they walked back to the baseline after a point

2. How they held their heads and shoulders (the power of posture)

3. Where they focused their eyes

4. The pattern of their breathing

5. Their self-talk

The best athletes in the world focus more on what they are doing when they are *not* playing than they do on what they do when they are playing.

Why?

Because the key to high performance is to manage your energy. The best tennis players understood the concept of energy hyper-renewal and hyper-recovery – routines that enabled them to get their mind, body, spirit, and emotions right in a matter of 15-20 seconds in between points. How fascinating and applicable for every person, athlete or not, who performs in anything.

Teach your athletes this concept by sharing the research study with them about what the best tennis players in the world do *in between points*. Draw the parallels for *your* sport. Then have them do a little writing exercise.

Mental Preparedness: How Will I Act Between Points?

How should I walk or move in between plays, points, goals, etc.? Fast to get myself pumped up and excited? Slow to calm myself down when needed?

_____

_____

_____

How will I keep my posture in between plays, points, goals, etc.?
Walk tall? Never put my head down?

_____

_____

_____

Where will I focus my eyes in between plays, points, goals, etc.?
Straight ahead to stay in the zone? Look up to the sky?

_____

_____

_____

How will I control my breathing in between plays, points, goals, etc.? Fast paced when I need to get pumped up? Slow, controlled, deep breaths when I need to calm myself down?

_____

_____

_____

How will I talk to myself in between plays, points, goals, etc.? Tell myself positive things when things are not going well? Do I have little phrases I can remind myself of? What about when things are going great? When I get taken out of the game? When a guy or girl on the other team is trying to get under my skin?

_____

_____

_____

227

The best athletes are intentional. They plan how they will act and who they want to be *before* competition starts.

Coaches, you will have to really work hard to ensure this becomes part of your culture. The implications are massive when you prioritize mental game preparedness training into your practices!

Lesson 4:

OVERCOMING SELF-DOUBTS
BY REFRAMING YOUR THOUGHTS

Self-doubts cripple your athletes. They can make a great player look like a rookie. This lesson is mission critical.

"I should have done this instead of that."

"I should have taken that shot."

"He is way faster than me."

"I won't be able to stand my ground. She's going to knock me over."

"I'm not going to get the time I need to."

"I'm not going to score on this penalty kick."

These are the things that go through your athlete's mind. They come directly from real life answers that hundreds of student-athletes have answered when I take them through the "Overcoming Self-Doubt" exercise.

The next step is to *reframe* these false, unhelpful thoughts into something true and helpful.

Self-Doubt

"I should have done this instead of that."

Reframe

"I just learned what *not to do*. Move on, the next play will be better."

Self-Doubt

"I should have taken that shot. I am going to mess up again next time."

Reframe

"I'll shoot next time I am open. No big deal."

Self-Doubt

"He is way faster than me. Beats me every time and will likely beat me again."

Reframe

"I'll beat him by playing smarter, staying focused, and looking for my opportunities."

Self-Doubt

"I won't be able to stand my ground. She's going to knock me over."

Reframe

"I'll beat her with speed, quickness, and agility. Plus, I've been training, I am strong."

The self-doubts are the way these things are playing out in your athlete's subconscious thoughts. They are not *consciously* thinking about these things, but they *are there*. I've gone deep into the minds of over 50 athletes with this exercise and have pulled it out of them. They didn't even know the negative thoughts that they were having.

If you think this exercise is silly and simple, you are right. But it works. It is amazing when someone gets their doubts *out* of their head and onto paper. Everything changes. The PDF exercise can be found at www.andrewjsimpson.com/book-insider.

Lesson 5:

ENERGY AND ENTHUSIASM

Two Secret Ingredients to Gain the Mental Edge.

In 1979, Earvin "Magic" Johnson stepped onto the NBA scene as part of the L.A. Lakers, joining the likes of NBA greats Jamaal Wilkes, Norm Nixon, and of course, Kareem Abdul-Jabbar.

The rookie was ecstatic. He had a natural bounce to his step. He had an extra dose of *energy and enthusiasm* compared to the rest of the team.

After games, Johnson would be sprinting around, jumping up and down, fist bumping his teammates and throwing haymaker high fives. Kareem and the other veterans were unamused. "Rookie," they would say as they shook their heads in mockery.

But over the course of the season, something "magical" started to happen. Magic's energy and enthusiasm became *contagious,* just as most great things naturally become overtime.

He stayed true to his belief that the team and the world needed more E&E to be successful. If you're happy and you know it....

By the end of the season it was reported that Kareem and the rest of the team were *different*. They would join Magic in the excitement rather than mocking or criticizing him for it.

As simple as it sounds, one of the reasons your athlete or team is underperforming is because their energy stinks and/or their enthusiasm is non-existent. The players who have a natural dose of it are suppressing it, scared of being judged by the unenthusiastic teammates. No one wants to stand out, yet everyone wants to be outstanding. It just does not work that way.

A common denominator of successful athletes and successful teams is that they display a genuine *enthusiasm* for their sport. They get *excited* about practice, about games, and about the opportunity to get better. They also get *excited* for their teammates.

Their energy is also positive. It is joyful. They are responsible for the energy they bring to practice each day. If they are having an off day, they tell somebody. They know that the worst thing a teammate can do is bring negative energy into a room because it brings down morale.

Take your athletes through the following exercise. Encourage the ones you know have good energy to *bring it out more often*. Share the story of Magic Johnson.

Energy and Enthusiasm Exercise

Do you like hanging out with or playing sports with people whose energy STINKS and who have ZERO enthusiasm?

YES   NO

When you have good, positive energy, you typically feel and perform better.

TRUE   FALSE

Sometimes you **HOLD BACK** enthusiasm to match the enthusiasm of others around you (if they aren't enthusiastic, YOU aren't either).

TRUE   FALSE

Energy and enthusiasm are the two secret keys that unlock FULL potential in every area of life.

3 STEPS TO MORE E&E

Step 1

What holds me back from being more energetic and enthusiastic? What holds me back from being my true?

Examples:

Bigger personalities around me

My self-limiting beliefs → *"I am just not an enthusiastic person"*

I will be judged if I have positive energy

_____

_____

_____

What do I do to overcome these fears faster so I can be more energetic and enthusiastic?

Example: get more excited when others do well, cheer for them and their successes

Smile more, bring joy to practice

Tell a teammate that I am going to be more positive and enthusiastic because it is who I am and it is the best thing for the team

_____

_____

_____

Step 2

If I have more positive and consistently high energy, and show genuine enthusiasm for all aspects of my life, what will the result be?

Example: the team will win more

I will enjoy practice and games more

My teammates will be more motivated

My coaches will be happier

_____

_____

_____

Lesson 6:

ACTING MEDIUM

Tony Dungy, former head coach of the Indianapolis Colts, taught me the concept of *acting medium*. I now have passed it on to all of my mindset coaching students and we discuss it a couple times a year with our athletes at PFP during motivational messages. It's amazing the lightbulbs that go off.

It was a concept he used to produce a Super Bowl winning team, and more importantly, champion caliber *people*. He found that most athletes have trouble **controlling their emotions.**

What goes up must come down. When something goes down, it takes a lot of energy to get back up. Acting medium is the best way to maintain consistent, peak performance. If your athlete (or team if you are a coach) struggles with consistent *results,* I can guarantee you they have inconsistent *feelings and emotions.*

Acting Medium Exercise

During practice, how are my emotions? Do I get super pumped up when I score at *practice?* Do I get super angry when I make a mistake at *practice? Write about my emotions at practice below.*

_____

_____

_____

_____

During games, how do I act when things go wrong? When I make a mistake? Ref makes a terrible call? My teammates are slacking? Coach pulls me out? I get a penalty unfairly?

_____

_____

_____

_____

ACTING MEDIUM

When things go poorly, the best athletes stay calm, cool, and collected. They do not let their emotions get overly *high* when things go well, nor do they let themselves get too *low* when things are not going well.

They understand that acting medium is the key to *consistent, high performance.*

How do I need to act moving forward? Why?

_____

_____

_____

_____

Use this exercise to bring self-awareness to your child's performance. It can be used for school, sports, or anything else that causes their emotions to rollercoaster.

I recommend that you take a moment to think about the ups and downs in your life. Reflect on the good that came from the downs.

And remember: as the leader, the parent, or the coach, that the way *you* respond to the ups and downs of sport and life will often be the determining factor for how your athlete will respond.

GETTING OUT OF YOUR HEAD AND INTO THE ZONE

What does being in your head really mean?

W hat that really means is that they are having negative or unhelpful thoughts and/or feelings.

Negative thoughts and feelings include:

- He or she is faster than me. I won't be able to keep up.

- I did not practice well this week. This isn't going to go well.

- My wrist is bothering me. I might not do well today (pre-excuse building).

- I really hope I start today. I hope coach plays me.

- I can't believe I just turned the ball over with two minutes to go. I might have just cost the team the game.

- I missed a wide-open shot!

The list goes on and on. Identifying the negative thoughts or feelings is the pre-work you have to do before you ever learn to get out of your head.

By the way, it is impossible to be *in your head* and *in the zone* at the same time. So let's figure out how we can help our athletes build confidence, competence, and courage needed to do so.

Four-Part Formula for Getting Out of Your Head and into the Zone

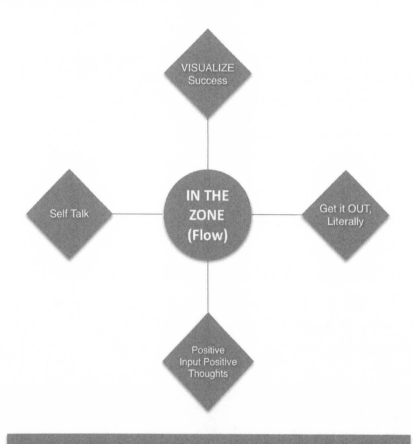

It is difficult to share everything about the implementation of this four-part formula. If you go to www.andrewjsimpson.com/book-insider you will be able to access the entire webinar, worksheets, and how to coach this formula. And if you want to go deeper and get individualized coaching, email me directly at andrew@pfpfit.com. I'd be happy to coach you through it.

PRE-WORK

Before your athlete goes through the four steps, you as the parent or coach must recognize your role in your athlete(s) being in their head.

Do you give them too many pre-game, in-game, or post-game reminders and critiques? Wouldn't *you* overthink if somebody was constantly pouring *their thoughts* into your head?

Less is more. Fewer reminders, less instruction, less criticism. More praise, compliments, and calmness.

The Four-Part Formula

1. **Visualize success: we teach our athletes the power of visualization.**

   We have them practice vividly picturing what they want to happen in a game situation.

   How do you want to play? Close your eyes and picture that every day. It's like a muscle, it gets stronger and more effective as you train it.

   There was a story of a coach who did an experiment with his basketball team. He had 15 players and broke them up into three groups. Group one visualized shooting and making 100 free throws at the end of practice for six straight weeks. Group two shot 100 free throws for the six weeks. Group three shot 50 and *visualized 50.*

   The results? Group one improved their free throw percentage by 7%. Group two, 9%. Group three, 12%!

   The point is that your players can begin playing better today without even practicing their sport. Seven percent is pretty good for not picking up a ball!

In the workbook we have a few exercises that will help your athletes take this from concept to action.

2. **Get out of your head, literally. "If you don't *let* it out, you will *act* it out."**

We teach our athletes to express their stinkin' thinkin'. Expression is one of the human needs to be fully happy. Express your negative thoughts about the play you made. Express your negative feelings about the coach pulling you out (don't gossip, talk to the coach).

If you keep it in your head, you'll *never* be in the zone. Writing it down is the other option (but not as effective).

3. **Positive input, positive thinking.**

Whatever is going into your brain via social media, the people you hang out with, and your teachers will determine your thoughts. If I watch *Desperate Housewives of New Jersey* every night as opposed to watching a TED Talk, my thoughts will become very different. We forget that our input determines our output.

Think about it. Why were we the way we were when *we* were teenagers? Because of the input we received from our parents, coaches, and peers. The challenge nowadays is that more input than ever is coming from celebrities, social media "influencers," and friends.

Want a couple of action steps for you and/or your athletes?

Hang out with more positive people if you want more positive thoughts. Unfollow negative, unhelpful social media people if you find yourself being too negative. Watch TED Talks by guys like John Wooden if you are a coach who thinks they could benefit from thinking more like him. Have your *team* read books together by guys like Jon Gordon. Input determines output.

If you are *in your head* and not liking the chatter you are hearing, change what is going *into your head.*

4. Self-Talk Prep

It is one thing to tell yourself "you've got this" when something negative or unfortunate happens. But that is *reactive*. Instead, tell yourself every single morning who you are going to become. "I am *positive*. I am *courageous*. I am a *leader*."

It is one thing to try to psych yourself up *when* something goes poorly in a game by saying, "C'mon, you can do it. Stay focused." But that is also reactive.

We teach our athletes to *pre-plan* the self-talk.

If coach pulls me out of the game, *this* is what I will tell myself.

If I mess up in a game or have a bad turnover, *this* is what I will tell myself.

If I am performing below my potential, *this* is the reminder I'll give myself.

Self-talk prep is preparing what you will say beforehand rather than reacting. As a society, we are not good at being proactive. As coaches, we can *teach* young athletes how to do so. But remember, it starts with you.

A quick lesson on being nervous

Athletes play better when they transfer their *natural nerves* to excitement rather than fear. See below.

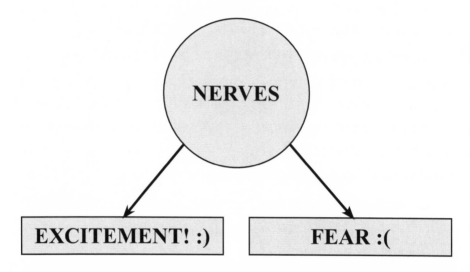

What I love about this visual is that athletes, especially the *visual athletes,* can immediately benefit from this during their next bout with fear. When they start to feel nervous, they can, in their minds, send those nerves to the **left** towards EXCITEMENT, rather than fear!

Shared Learning

I first learned about shared learning back in 2014 at a mentorship conference I attended. The teacher had us write down answers to different self-reflection type questions. The writing piece created clarity, which was helpful. But even more helpful than *writing* down answers was *sharing them out loud* with one, two, or a group of people.

Teens do not like this *initially*, which may be a hang-up for you as the coach. However, teens do not like it *before they do it*. No one likes the unknown. Once they engage in this type of learning and begin communicating with their peers on a deeper level than "what's up," they begin to enjoy it.

Why? Because we are relational beings created for connection. That includes millennials, Gen X, Gen Y, all the "gens."

It will take practice, but if you commit to doing *shared learning* once you start implementing more Mindset Performance Coaching into your routine, you will see your student-athletes open up, break through, smile more, and ultimately witness a more unified and cohesive team form before your eyes. I recommend doing it in partners to start, then small groups, then out loud to the entire team.

Go to www.andrewjsimpson.com/book-insider to download the entire library of Mental Game Ready Exercises.

LIFE-READY
MENTAL PREPAREDNESS

This section is by far my favorite. Life-ready mental preparedness is amplified personal growth for teens. It is great to overcome mistakes in a game or overcome your self-doubts about going up against a bigger, faster athlete. However, discovering who you are, why you matter, being confident in who you are, learning what makes you tick, deciding who you want to become and why, and proactively choosing the character and legacy you want to leave behind is so, so much more impactful and transformational.

Going through these exercises with your athletes as well as sharing *your* personal answers is tough in the beginning. It is uncomfortable. But like my friend Joe once said, "If you don't feel like you are going to throw up at least once a month, you are too comfortable."

I had preconceived notions prior to doing this as a coach. "Will these types of exercises be well-received by the athletes?" I wondered. I thought maybe some would like them, but most would roll their eyes.

I was wrong. These kids are *craving* personal growth and development. They want to learn about themselves. They want to become more confident. They want someone to call out the very things they are all thinking and struggling with. It makes them feel more accepted.

The problem is that they do not have any opportunities to do this – until now. You can change that for them by administering the following "Life Ready Mental Preparedness Exercises."

Old School Becomes New School

Remember from before:

Beliefs → Thoughts → Feelings → Actions → Habits → Character (Who you are)

If there was a class in school called *"How to become the most confident, courageous, successful leader you can be,"* our youth would be in better shape. I will likely get criticism for this, but I truly do believe this is more important than history, mathematics, science, and even English. Physical Education would fall in line as well.

The curriculum could read something like this:

Week 1-2:	What are your gifts, strengths, interests, and passions
Week 3-4:	What kind of person do you want to become
Week 5-6:	What kind of person do you not what to become
Week 7-8:	Vulnerability: what do you need to change and work on as a person
Week 9-10:	Success and Confidence: defining what it is and what it means to you
Week 11-12	Goal setting and Intentionality: taking action to improve your life

Each week we would share stories of people who were lost and scared, but now confident and successful. People learn best from stories. We would share analogies and examples to help kids come up with concrete strengths. There would be accountability and action steps for when they got home. Lord knows we need more accountability! How do you identify strengths and weaknesses? Ask the people around you who love you.

We would have calendars and timelines for goal setting so that we didn't get distracted and jump to the next goal without accomplishing the first. Obviously, there would be a lot of shared learning.

I am not a traditional teacher, but I am a teacher. We have taught thousands of kids that "curriculum" from above. For the majority of them, whether they are 12 years old or 20, it is the first time they have ever heard the concepts or done the written exercises.

Maybe it is *not* the first time they heard it. Maybe a parent taught them one time. There are two problems with this:

1. People need to hear things seven different times from multiple people, at different stages in their life, in order to really "hear it."

2. If I had a dollar for every time I have heard from a parent, "When I say it, it goes in one ear and out the other. When a coach says it, it sticks," I would be a very rich man.

I fear that far too many coaches and teachers are not yet equipped to teach this kind of material, the "life coaching" type of material that has mindset transforming power.

Just because you have never thought about this type of mentoring and coaching for your athletes doesn't mean it is too late to start. You can start today by prioritizing these lessons into your practices or trainings and begin to watch your kids increase their confidence and success exponentially.

Life Ready Exercise 1: CORE VALUES

"When you do not know who you are,
others will pressure you to fit into their mold."
-- RICK WARREN

Everything begins with having a clear set of your own unique core values. We went deep on this earlier. When you fail to have clear values, you make poor decisions. You feel uncertain and unconfident more often than not. The opposite of having core values and living by them is conforming and trying to be someone you are not. As the coach or the leader, it is imperative that you *first* create yours. That way you can facilitate the exercise.

As a person, this is what is most important to me in my life:

Examples: leading my family to be kind, loving, helpful people; volunteering my time and serving homeless people; spending quality time with my husband and creating memories with the family; tapping into my full God-given potential and using the fullness of my gifts and talents

1. _____

2. _____

3. _____

4. _____

5. _____

As a parent, this is what matters most to me for the future of my child:

Examples: modeling for my child what it looks like to be selfless and generous; helping my child to give their all in all they do and work hard; my child's mental and emotional well-being; my child's physical health and safety; showing my child what servant leadership looks like, how to be a person of influence and impact; my child's grades and effort in school

1. _____

2. _____

3. _____

4. _____

5. _____

As a coach, this is what matters most to me for the future of my athletes and teams:

Examples: modeling for them what it looks like to be a servant leader; seeing that they work hard and care more about the process than the outcome; helping them to see and value serving others above themselves; prioritizing communication with them and being real, authentic, and even vulnerable

1. _____

2. _____

3. _____

4. _____

5. _____

Now that you have written down your values, re-write them on the following lines and then write down the **"Red Light Habits"** you'll need to stop and **"Green Light Habits"** you'll need to start in order to begin living more congruent with the things you say are most important.

My Personal Values

Example: Value #1: volunteering my time and serving homeless people

Red light: I need to stop making excuses about how I don't have time. This is a value of mine. I will step down as president of the PTO and begin serving at the local shelter even though other parents may try to shame or condemn me.

Green light: contact the PTO and let them know my decision, and immediately contact the shelter or organization today and sign up for first day

1. _____

2. _____

3. _____

4. _____

5. _____

My Values as a Coach, Parent, or Teacher

Examples: Value #1: my athlete's grades and effort in school

Red light: put a stop to the extra sports activities causing my kid to get home at 9:30 p.m. and stay up until midnight just to finish homework.

Green light: spend the discretionary income on a world-class tutor instead of the private hitting coach

Red light and Green Light: Cut practice from two hours to 75 minutes of hyper-focused, high-intensity practice so they can have more time and energy to focus on grades. I need to send the right message. Just because other coaches practice two hours doesn't mean it is the only way.

1. _____

2. _____

3. _____

4. _____

5. _____

Set Your Past on Fire

The values exercise made me realize that by definition, I had been a hypocrite for many years as a coach. I did not know what I did not know. No one likes to admit it, but we all need to. We have all made decisions in our past that were misaligned with our values.

It is time to put the past in the past.

We *must* set our pasts on fire. You *must* empower and encourage your kids to set *their* pasts on fire. So many are holding on to regret, shame, and guilt. It is killing their confidence, and consequently, their performance. I know too many people who cannot sleep at night do to holding onto things they cannot change.

Values-based living is the only road to true success and regret-free living.

Set your past on fire and step into a new day. Get clear on your values and watch the stress, anxiety, fear, doubt, and insecurities begin to melt away. Choose to care more about what is right and less about what *others* say is right.

Be more mindful and thoughtful when making a decision about what to spend your time and money on for your athletes. Put first things first and give your best energy and attention to the things in life that give you a strong return on your investment.

This is a lesson for you, me, and all the kids we work with.

Life Ready Exercise 2: Role Models.

Becoming the kind of person you were always meant to be

For the past year, I have mentored a 13-year-old young man named John. This is the one-on-one *Mindset Performance Coaching (MPC)* we've been talking about throughout the book.

One of the lessons we do after trust is established is called "**Role Models:** Becoming the kind of person you were always meant to be."

It helps students identify the kind of person they were created to be based on passions and strengths. But equally important, it helps them identify the person they do *not* want to be, which can be eye opening when one realizes they are on the path to becoming that.

The first question is, "What kind of person do you want to see your younger brother or sister turn out to be?" If they are an only child, then sibling is replaced with best friend or a kid from a younger sports team that may look up to him or her.

Because teenagers sometimes have a limited vision for this kind of stuff or trouble articulating what is going on in their brains, I facilitate this by giving them specific examples.

"Do you want your younger brother to turn out to be a negative, unconfident person?" Their answer is "no" 99 out of 100 times, which by default means that they want to see their brother become a positive, optimistic, confident young man who believes in himself.

"Do you want your younger sister to turn out to be a bad listener who doesn't show an interest in what others are saying?"

What about a person who lets fear keep them from trying new things, from setting big, scary, ambitious goals?

Do you want your sister to turn out to be a follower? What about a gossiper, or someone who only gives her best effort in the things she enjoys?"

Light bulbs start to go off.

"No. I want my sister to be a kind, courteous person who is a good listener. I want her to run *through* her challenges fearlessly rather than shying away from them. I want her to dream big and set big goals! I want her to be a leader. I really hope she does not become a gossiper. And I definitely want her to give her best effort in everything she does. It's the right thing to do."

Next question: **Are you *being* the role model that *shows* your younger sibling the way to act in order to become that kind of person?**

If not, where are you failing to lead by example?

Most of us do more for other people than we do for ourselves.

And finally, we end with one final critically important question:

Are You Prepared to Become Just Like Mom and Dad?

Years ago, I noticed some characteristics and habits about my parents that I did not love. I think we *all* have those. I was about 23 years old and I decided to write down all the qualities, good and bad, about my parents. They don't know about me doing this, but I am sure they would applaud me for it now. And I *guarantee* they wish *they* would have done this when they were my age too – or even younger.

I will not reveal all the qualities I wrote down about them. But I will summarize it by first telling you that there were some *really good ones* that I want to adopt and continue on in my own life.

My dad was always present. He always showed up. He called me just about every day to say, "Hey bud, just checkin' in. What are you up to? How's your day?"

My mom has always been a good listener. She didn't care *what* we were telling her about, she just wanted to spend time with us and hear what we had to say.

And then there were those qualities and characteristics that I was not so fond of. I made a decision that day that I would actively and relentlessly work to be the exact opposite of those few characteristics I did not admire.

Would you agree that this is a good exercise to do with young men and women? The athletes on your team? Your children?

If you are a coach and you have a few athletes that are negative and reluctant to help other teammates, it could be that they watched their mom or dad display that same behavior for 13 years prior.

Don't forget this truth: that most of our youth's behaviors *are learned*.

To help that young man or woman *identify, decide, and correct* their behavior could change their life forever. On the other hand, be careful because critiquing and condemning their bad behavior breeds defensiveness. This is what "every adult does," in their minds.

Helping *them* become awake to their flaws and empowering them to decide on a new behavior will lead them to *thanking* you down the road. It's a minor difference in approach, but it has a major impact in their response. *How* you say it matters most.

I took a female collegiate athlete through this exercise during the summer of 2019. She realized that growing up in her home, it was not acceptable to talk about feelings. Her mom and dad kept silent when they were upset with one another. They did not talk about their emotions at all. She was trying to find the source of her anxiety and the reason she was constantly "in her own head."

Well, if you do not let it out of your mouth, there is only one place for it to stay stuck – in your head.

"If you do not let it out, you'll act it out," I told her. "Did your parents act out their feelings more than they spoke them?"

"Yes", she sobbed. "I do not want that to be my path. I am going to start letting it out no matter what."

Lead your students to more "A-HA!" moments.

I could have made the mistake with John by coming right out with, "What qualities do you want to change or improve that you may have received from mom or dad?" He may have never had a breakthrough if I'd done it this way.

Instead I said, "John, you have already mentioned you want to become a more positive, optimistic person. I am going to ask you a tough question. How does your dad respond when things are not going his way? Does he have a tendency to be negative? Pessimistic? Does he easily get frustrated?" When I framed it that way, he was able to answer the question directly opposed to broadly.

Coach's note: It is important to seed the conversation with a statement like the one below so that the kids you are working with do not end up having ill feelings or resentment towards their parents:

"John, no one is perfect and even IF your dad does have a tendency to be negative, it doesn't mean he is a negative person. I guarantee he loves you and would want to see you become a more positive person and learn from his example. It doesn't make him a bad guy, it just means he may have never learned what you are learning right now, which is to learn from your parents."

Every person has undesirable qualities, tendencies, and habits. I believe that can and should stop with that generation, but it never does. This exercise is a start.

We need to learn from our parents, and even our parent's parents.

John, without me probing, added that he did not like that his dad yelled a lot at him and his siblings. He did not like the fact that his dad was a "glass half empty guy." He did not like that his dad was stressed out and frustrated most nights after work. He did not like the fact that his dad's mood and attitude seemed to change with the blowing of the wind. Lastly, he couldn't stand hearing his dad preach, "Keep your head up. Stay positive," on the sports field. "Hypocritical" was an accurate description.

Wow! What breakthrough moments. This kid's life has been and will be changed forever because he decided who he did *not* want to become. And by default, he chose who he *did* want to become.

We are showing him the way to be more positive by identifying negative thoughts and tendencies. We are showing him the way to avoid *unnecessary* stress and overwhelm that comes at the expense of his health and happiness. We are teaching him about priorities, values, and goal setting.

Why are we doing this? Because if we focus on the root, the fruit will come. If John becomes more positive, he will be a better teammate. If he becomes more positive, adversity will not crush his attitude and spirit. If he becomes a more optimistic person, he will become a better athlete. He will take coach's criticism a little better. He will work harder at practice believing that the long-term payoff will be worth it – *all because of an exercise in which he was given the life-changing opportunity to spend time and energy thinking about role models.*

I know you may be thinking, "Where on earth will I find time to do that with all of my athletes?"

Start with one a day. One a week. This book is not for the coach who looks for excuses. This book is for the coach who is committed to strengthening the minds, winning the hearts, and inspiring the souls of their athletes.

We could have spent that 30 minutes working on John's core strength and speed, but I already told you that I value both emotional resiliency and personal well-being *above* physical performance enhancement.

And since values deserve the *best and first part* of your time, energy, and attention, I prioritized this writing exercise for John *before* working on the other stuff.

The result? John's life got better, as opposed to just his upcoming season.

A quick note about immediate gratification:

Sport skill development and athletic development provide visible progress. Sweat drips down the face. The body is tired. Muscles get fatigued. You *know and can see* stuff is happening. Mindset strengthening, emotional fitness improvement, those things take longer, but what may not always be easy, convenient, or immediately gratifying is definitely *worth it.*

Life Ready Exercise 3: Strengths, Gifts, and Talents that Last

When I was a high school fool, this is what I thought my strengths were limited to:

- **Good at getting good grades without trying**
- **A good football player**
- **A good basketball player**
- **Able to jump high**
- **Popular with girls (some may argue that I was delusional, which may be true)**

Here is the deal. I have met way too many insecure, uncertain, and unconfident kids due to an inadequate effort on my part in helping them to discover their true strengths – what *actually* matters.

What matters to teenagers?

I share this with our athletes regularly:

"Isn't it odd that when you are in middle school and high school, the only things that matter are:

1. Being good at sports

2. Being book smart

3. Looking good and feeling good about your popularity and status

The minute you leave high school, literally none of those things matter anymore."

This is a quick, fruitful reminder for your kids.

What happens if we do not correct this messed up mindset while they are teens? These three "desired strengths" shift into three similar desired strengths in adulthood.

1. I want to be good at making money and I want to acquire nice things (I'll find my worth in my car, my house, and my vacations).

2. I want *everyone* to like me and accept me, no matter the cost or conformity (people's opinions of me matter most)

3. I want to achieve high "positions" and statuses in jobs and other arenas

These are three empty, disappointing things to strive for - things that help no one but yourself. These are three targets that never stop moving. Kids who value sports, looks, and book smarts most will end up becoming adults who are discontent and feel worthless unless they are rich in money, possessions, and position.

Rachel's Story

Rachel was a senior in high school when she came to me with the question, "Coach Andrew, how do I know if I am insecure? And if I am, how do I fix it?"

Coach's note: *We are grateful that our athletes are vulnerable and trust us enough to ask us these types of questions. But the truth is, it was not always like this. We have worked hard to develop trusting relationships with our athletes because we know trust is the foundation of influence. One way is by taking communication courses and reading books on communication by great communicators.*

I told Rachel to spend a few days pondering that question and talking with God about it. I told her that it sounded like she *was* indeed insecure, but that she would need to find the root cause of her insecurities before she could go to work on them. Insecurities, after all, are made up in our minds, they are not physical things that harm us. We created them and we *can* get rid of them.

With some guidance, she discovered exactly why she was insecure. She was unaware of the multitude of *true strengths* that she had because those strengths were very seldom recognized or celebrated.

The truth is that Rachel has had the makeup of a highly confident and successful person for years. She is kind, caring, encouraging, and the kind of person who just makes you feel happier by being in their presence. She is mature in her attitude and response to adversity, she is able to communicate well with adults, and she is proactive with time management. The list goes on and on.

Yet she felt insecure because she did not have the genetic makeup of a "popular high school girl." She didn't dress like she was going to a club and did not have looks that high school guys were after. She also did not have a very attractive social media presence, meaning that she didn't post pictures of herself by the pool, she didn't post pictures of her kissing her boyfriend, and she didn't post pictures of herself playing sports.

You know what that actually tells me? She was very, very *secure*.

So secure that she did not feel the need to post things just to get likes or compliments from people she barely knew and who barely knew her. She had no clue how confident and awesome she really was because confidence and awesomeness in middle and high school is based on some of the dumbest, most short-sighted standards ever.

Regarding sports, she was not a standout athlete who would be going to college for sports. In regard to school, she got good grades, but she was pretty average there too.

Given all this, Rachel needed to hear something.

In fact, *every* middle and high school kid needs to hear something:

You will be insecure and unconfident *all* the days of your life until you decide to stop focusing on superficial, selfish ambitions and start to discover your unique, God-given strength that make you you and that allow you to be more helpful to *other people!*

Insecurity and a lack of understanding of who you are and who God created you to be is one of the biggest things holding kids back from their full potential – on the field, in the classroom, and in life.

Not knowing who you are and why you matter opens the door for your self-esteem to be shattered when adversity comes knocking. In order to help kids avoid this, call it out regularly. Remind them what matters most and prove it by what you recognize and reward. But first, take them through this exercise. Empower them through your words. Passionately profess the truth about *real strengths* and convince them that what matters most is *not* the scoreboard of looks, grades, or sports.

Exercise: What are my true strengths?

What are your Top 3-5 strengths? These are your God-given gifts, talents, and unique things about you! If your athletes are having trouble, tell them to think about what their parents, friends, and those closest to them would say if they were being completely open and honest with you. "What would my mom, dad, best friend, or coach say are my best qualities, talents, or strengths?"

Examples: I am a very determined worker; I do not give up; I am very kind and compassionate, maybe because I have been through tough times; I am very coachable; I am a great listener and communicator.

1. _____

2. _____

3. _____

4. _____

5. _____

Why do these 3-5 strengths matter most? What good could come from them?

1. _____

2. _____

3. _____

4. _____

5. _____

Spend time on this with them. Share yours with them. It is transformational when they realize that the gifts they possess that they never thought mattered are indeed the ones that will benefit them and others around them *most!* And of course, do some shared learning in a group setting if you want a culture of openness and inclusivity.

Myth: work on your weaknesses if you want to succeed.

Our society has cemented this myth into our brains.

We were given gifts for a reason. Or "talents," as *CliftonStrengths* calls them. These are the things ingrained in our DNA that we are *intuitively* good at. I am not going to go deep into this topic as there are multiple books written on it already that you should read, such as *StrengthFinder 2.0.*

Give some serious attention to what *you* are spending the bulk of your time and energy trying to improve upon. What are your *athletes* focusing on at practice? Hopefully they are not wasting too much time working on their individual weaknesses. The best coaches help their players amplify their strengths and they only work on the weaknesses that they *must* get better at. Do what you do best and "hire" the rest.

Life Ready Exercise 4: Confidence

There is a fundamental flaw in the way your athletes view confidence. Until they change their *definition of confidence,* they will likely experience Rollercoaster Confidence. No one wants rollercoaster confidence – rollercoasters are fun when they are fun, but they also make people throw up.

What is confidence, really?

Confidence:

1) The belief in one's ability to do something

2) The feeling of self-assurance arising from one's appreciation of their abilities or qualities

3) The state of feeling certain about the truth of something

There are so many different definitions of confidence. How do you rate *your* confidence levels, then? As a parent or coach, how do you really determine if you kids are growing in their confidence or not?

I always ask the kids I work with, "How do you believe you can increase your confidence?"

If they don't shrug and say, "I don't know," then they almost always say this:

"Umm, well, just believe in myself, I guess?"

To which I reply, "If it was that easy, wouldn't you feel more confident already?"

One of the best things you can do for the future of the athletes you parent or coach is to help them create their own definition of confidence, one that is within their control.

Confidence from The Scoreboard of Sports

Am I a starter?

Am I the best *scorer* on the team?

Did I get first team all-conference?

Did they talk about me in the newspaper article?

Did the captains on the team tell me I did a good job?

Did my coach share my accomplishments with the rest of the team?

Are my parents proud of my results? My statistics?

If these are the things you believe have to happen *before* you become confident and feel good about yourself, I need to let you in on a little secret.

You will never be fully and consistently confident. You will experience Rollercoaster Confidence all the time. This happens when you put too much weight on things you cannot control 100%.

The confidence exercise will be a game changer for you and your athletes.

Exercise: Confidence

What is your definition of confidence?

Have them write it out. This step is important.

What *currently* dictates your confidence?

Examples:

- *I feel confident when I am playing well.*
- *I feel confident when I do something right.*
- *I feel confident when I get a great score.*
- *I feel confident when I look awesome.*
- *I feel confident when I get a good grade.*
- *I feel confident when I receive a compliment from parents or a coach.*
- *I feel confident when I prepare for a test by studying.*

1. _____

2. _____

3. _____

4. _____

5. _____

6. _____

The problem with the list above is that I cannot control those things. If I keep using those for confidence, my confidence will always be like a rollercoaster.

Redefining how I determine my own self-confidence:

Examples of redefining your confidence:

I will feel more confident when…

1. I have trained and prepared well for a game.

2. I finish what I start.

3. I am seeking out help and guidance.

4. I seek to relate to another who isn't like me.

5. I know I did the right thing, even though it was hard.

6. I have trouble with something and ask the coach for help and make progress.

7. I know I am doing something well, and even though the coach isn't watching, I can still feel good about what I am doing.

8. I take care of my physical appearance as best as I can, and I am at peace that everyone has a different opinion on looks.

9. I know I have studied.

From this day forward, these are the things that will determine if I feel confident or not.

1. _____

2. _____

3. _____

4. _____

5. _____

6. _____

7. _____

8. _____

Important things to understand:

1. Having a new view of confidence will be challenged by the way other people determine confidence.

2. This change will not happen overnight.

3. If you never look at this lesson again, it will be meaningless.

4. If you work hard at this, you will become the most confident, positive, successful person and athlete you can possibly become.

We tell our athletes all the time, "Your coach chooses if you are a starter or not. You can *influence* this, but you cannot *control it*. If you *have* to be a starter to feel confident, prepare to not feel confident or good about yourself at times. Your teachers give you your final grades. You cannot control the number. Base your confidence on your effort."

And you will need to remind your athletes from time to time that **effort is not** simply how hard you work. It is working hard *and* smart.

And I need to remind you once more how critically important it is that you teach your athletes these things during *non-conflict* times. People do not learn well when they feel like they are being called out for something they did wrong.

Not every athlete was created to be a *scorer.*

Some were designed to be the best defensive players. Some were created to be the source of positivity, light, and hope on the team. Some were made to be the Robin to Batman on the team – a great *complementary player.* Can you imagine how confident and successful your players and teams will be once they truly understand and own this concept?

The Confidence Competence Loop

> *"Confident people become that way by doing everything within their control to be the best they can be."*
> -- Unknown

Confidence enhancement is one of the main pillars of our brand. We discovered, after thousands of conversations, that confidence was really the thing parents and athletes wanted to get out of training. Bigger, faster, and stronger was a means to the end, which was confidence.

We teach our athletes that confidence is not something you are born with, but rather something you *generate.*

You generate it by *doing confidence-generating things* day after day after day. When you improve in anything, your confidence muscles contract and get bigger. Which ones do you and your athletes need to start flexing more often?

"Johnny, did you know that you can become more confident in your shooting abilities today? You just need to *do* the things that will *lead* to you believing in your abilities more than you do right now!"

"Duh", Johnny said.

Johnny said duh, yet Johnny had not yet "done the duh."

Remember, common sense is not common practice.

Confident people were not born confident. The learned it and then generated it.

Confident people are simply willing to *do* the things that others are not willing to do.

Corey's Story

We work with an athlete named Corey. He is a 16-year-old lacrosse player who is very introverted, unsure of himself, and used to be scrawny.

He decided it would be a good idea to start strength training. Within 12 weeks, he put on roughly six pounds of muscle and people started noticing.

His confidence and belief in himself went through the roof. He started engaging in conversations with his coaches more. He started putting himself out there in social situations.

And he told me one day, "Thanks for having this place for me to come and work out at. It's inspiring. I love that you guys challenge me."

Was it the six pound of muscle that made him more confident?

Or was it subconscious confidence, just knowing that he was now doing something about his lack of strength and size leads to inner self-belief?

We improve our confidence the minute we decide to *do something* to improve an area of our life that needs improving.

What is it for you? For your athlete?

Not confident in your ability to dribble a basketball? Practice what you don't feel like working on *when you do not feel like it.*

Not confident in how you look? Hire a fitness trainer, eat better, and work out.

Not confident in your ability to ask a boy or girl out? *Go do it now. The feeling of confidence will never come until you do the thing you are unconfident in.*

Do the do that you don't want to do

Typically, the things that lead to us becoming more confident are the very things we do not want to do. If we wanted to do them, we would already be more confident. You need to do the do that you don't want to do. Confidence is on the other side of your fears and feelings of doubt and "I don't feel like it". Guess what you need to do? *Do it even when you do not feel like it!*

You Choose Your Misery

We had an athlete come in for his first session this past week. We had him do chin ups. He did four. He looked mad. I said to him, "Great job Taylor! You pushed out that last rep, way to not give up!"

"I stink at chin ups," he groaned, embarrassed to try again. His comparison to other people, about something that doesn't matter (chin ups), led to him having diminished confidence. WHAT!? That is insane.

"Well, it is a good thing that no awards are given out for best chin ups, nor does anyone really care how good you are at them. Have you ever thought about why you care so much about doing good at things that are insignificant and inconsequential?" I asked him.

He changed his outlook after that day. He began recognizing when he allowed the feelings of misery or worthlessness to pop up from things that honestly, do not matter much.

Our teens need to be reminded that they cannot control how tall they are, the color of their eyes, whether or not they have acne, if they have to wear eyeglasses, or any other physical attribute they were given by God.

The scoreboard of *looks,* for example, is based on things that we cannot control, which is pretty absurd if you ask me. I get passionate about this stuff when I talk with our athletes. I look them dead in the eye and tell them that they do not have to deal with the head trash that I know is floating around in their minds. That they do not have to live with the feelings of fear, doubt, and insecurity any longer.

"I don't know if you are really hearing me, athlete. If you are going to become the most confident version of you, you have to change what you care about and what you will allow to rock your confidence" I tell them.

We have to help our athletes change what they care about.

This is why at age 23 I decided to start basing my own self-worth on the opinion of one person and one person only - God. He created me the way he wanted me to look for a reason, and I trust that.

I joke with my athletes sometimes and give the following "speech."

"Do not take this personally, but I don't really trust your opinions. I bet you are a great person, but if you tell me I am ugly or unattractive, it will not affect my levels of confidence and my belief in myself. It may make me question myself for a split second, but I have changed how I *think* about attractiveness. Your opinion will not make me feel worse about myself, I assure you.

I understand *why* you might think I am unattractive, and it is because you are just going along with what everyone else has determined is the standard for beauty or ugliness. You are entitled to your opinion of my looks, but last I checked, you are not God. So your opinion is *yours*, it is *not* reality and it is *not* the almighty truth.

I've decided that your opinion of me is not *my* reality. It's yours. When someone judges you, yells at you, criticizes you, is impatient with you, or makes fun of you, you must understand one important truth: **people's opinions are a reflection of *their own* thoughts, experiences, and beliefs. What is true to *them* does not have to be true to *you*.**" #youdecide

You can inspire *unshakable confidence* in your athletes. There are few things more rewarding than seeing a *teenager* stand away from the crowd and embrace their awesomeness.

Big Self, Little Self

We all have had moments in our lives that we *wish* we would have stepped up. We wish we would have stepped up and said something or done something that *should have* been said or done. But we didn't. We may have regrets or potential that was never realized because of this.

BIG SELF vs. **LITTLE** SELF

When you are being your **LITTLE SELF?**

- You let the fear of the unknown stop you from stepping up. "If I do that, it might have a negative result."

- You let the fear of being judged keep you from standing up for what you know is right or what you believe in.

- You wait for *someone else* to do something or say something that you know needs to be done or said. ("Why does it have to be me? I'm sure someone else will help my teammates who is struggling.")

- You have regrets because you know you could have made a difference if you'd just stepped up.

When you are being your **BIG SELF?**

- You feel it in your *gut* that you need to do something or say something, and then you *do!*

- You take action quickly; you do not overthink it. You run *through* fear because you know that you cannot go over, under, or around it.

- You do the thing or say the thing because it will help someone else, even if it means other people might judge you.

- You lead. You choose the path less traveled.

When I learned this concept, it was a breakthrough moment in my life. I was nervous to share my message about the problem in youth sports today. I was apprehensive about lovingly telling a parent that their current approach is killing their kid's confidence. I feared that coaches would not respect my views, that they would think my ideas about youth athletic development were dumb. I also feared sharing my faith.

So what did I do? I justified my little self. Every time I let my little self come out, I made an excuse as to why.

"I don't want to offend anyone." (Coward.)

"It's not worth saying anything; they will not listen anyway." (Coward.)

"I need to learn more. I need to wait a little bit longer. Eventually I'll be ready to share." (Coward.)

Teach your team, your athlete, or even your spouse the concept of Big Self and Little Self. Then commit to overcoming cowardice and stepping up and into the best version of yourself.

The only thing that will overcome your Little, Cowardly Self is your Big, Courageous Self. The same is true for your athletes. Define what that is for them, then take them through a pre-practice mindset writing exercise. If you want more leaders on your team, this is worth the 10-minute sacrifice.

EXERCISES FOR THE COACH

In this section of Part 4, "Putting it into Practice," I wanted to include a few exercises I have seen help coaches increase their influence and impact. There is also one for parents, which you will find to be indirectly helpful to you if you are not a parent, and directly impactful if you are. Enjoy this section, I believe it will change the game.

Coach Lesson #1: Root BEFORE fruit, always!

The apples on that tree symbolize the sports accomplishments, the intelligence, and the popularity. They symbolize the wins, the state championships, and the accolades.

Guess what happens if you stare at apples all day long? Guess what happens when you spend your effort and energy thinking about how good they would taste if you had the apples?

The tree will die and the apples will go bad. Why? Because you were focused on the wrong thing – the fruit.

The *roots* are what need the best of your attention. You need to water them, take care of them, and work on them every single day. The roots are the following things:

Athlete:

- Best effort at the drills you hate doing
- Watching game film weekly
- Getting to the gym to lift 3x/week
- Stretching and foam rolling to recover
- Kind and courteous gestures towards your teammates
- Asking coach for help

Coach:

- Best effort at the drills you hate coaching
- Organizing team strength training and sticking to it
- One-on-one meetings with your players consistently
- Texting, calling, and checking in with your players just to see how they're doing
- Mentoring them, helping them become better at life
- Mental game exercises every single week without fail

These are just a few of the examples of the *roots*. The reason we don't focus on them with enough passion and vigor is because they are *unseen*. They do not produce immediate fruit – but the results *are* proven. They *will* lead to fruit if you just *stick to it,* which requires another level of what we call "stick-to-it-ive-ness."

What if the *apples* never come, though?

I ask our athletes, "What if you *never* become liked, accepted, and popular? What if you *never* become as good at sports as your best friend or rival? What if you *never* get straight As or get a college scholarship?"

What *if* your team loses more than they win? What *if* you end up with some bad apples on the team who mess things up? What *if* parents, administration, or other critics do what they do best and *criticize you?*

What if? You tell me. What would *really* happen if the fruit doesn't come?

Nothing. Nothing will happen. You'll keep going and keep growing. You will keep watering the root, working on it daily, and sow new seeds if a new tree is needed. But remember, proven roots produce proven fruits. Just stay the course.

Ask your athletes, what "apples" you are looking to obtain in your life?

What does "working on the root" look like?

How consistently, intensely, and for how long will you need to work on the root to hopefully harvest the apples you want?

Coach Lesson #2: Creating a Team Theme

"Based on who you want to be and what you want to accomplish a year from now, what *theme* will support that journey?"

Our team theme at PFP in 2018 was "Root Before Fruit." Every Monday at our team meeting we would read it aloud. "Focus on the *root* and the *fruit* will come!"

It was our reminder to focus on what made us a great team and business to begin with. Building relationships, creating experiences, listening, going above and beyond for our guests, and learning and growing personally and professionally were some of those foundational pieces. Getting back to the root was key for us to get better.

What is your team theme?

I encourage you to create one for your team *and* your family. To get buy-in from your players (or family members), create the theme with them. Have a "theme session" where everyone thinks about their ideas for the theme, shares them aloud, and collectively decides on the one that makes the most sense to connect *where your team currently is* with *where you want to go.* Your yearly theme is the bridge between your past and future, where you are and where you want to be a year from now.

Coach Lesson #3: Consistency and Intensity

The two reasons your athletes will fail to realize their potential or reap the fruits of their labor is either a lack of *consistency* or a lack of *intensity*.

Consistency is how frequently we do something over time. Intensity represents *how* we do something.

We all understand consistency. Consistency alone will take an athlete from below average results to average or even above.

Why? Because "stick-to-it-ive-ness" is about as rare to find as a purple elephant.

If you can just stick to strength training for one year two times per week, you will put yourself into an elite class of people.

If you can commit to studying for your tests and going to tutoring for one full semester consistently, you'll blow your parents away with your grades.

Consistency will get you pretty darn far, but what exactly are you being consistent with? Do you need to upgrade *how* you are doing what you're doing to improve?

Honing Your How

When I went to college my freshman year to play basketball, I thought I was in great shape. After all, I had worked out and played basketball five or six days a week for the entire summer, and for a long time leading up to that summer.

I was very *consistent.*

When I got there, I noticed something about the *way* the upperclassmen were training and doing their skill development. Their *how* was honed.

How do you *hone your how?*

These guys were doing drills I had never seen at an intensity I did not know existed. In addition, they had their teammates filming them during their drills. I thought this was a little crazy and over the top.

That is what people say who really don't want to change, put in more work, or do what is needed to really take their game to another level. "That's over the top."

Intensity

If you want to become a world-class swimmer, avoid plateaus, experience *continual improvement,* and continually level up your results, it will take *far more* than swimming five days a week for two hours a day, year after year.

You will need to analyze your *intensity* and *hone your how.*

Here is an example of developing confidence through mastery:

Step 1: Have a coach assess and break down different parts of your swim. Your start, your turn, your arm action, leg action, and your breathing patterns.

Step 2: Analyze your skills out of water – your strength, explosiveness, speed, flexibility, endurance, nutrition, and sleep. Figure out which markers could be improved.

Step 3: Pick *one* aspect of your swim game that can be improved, watch film on it, study world-class swimmers, and go to town on that *one skill.* Do not try to do it all at once. When you try to do everything, you do nothing well.

Step 4: Have a coach coach you up on that skill, watch you, correct you, and time you until you see an improvement.

Step 5: Continue to work on the out-of-water skills, one at a time, along with your in-water skills.

Step 6: Repeat the steps above for another in-water and out-of-water skill.

Sounds exhausting right?

Don't be overwhelmed, *just pick one* if you are someone who wants to get better. Start working on *how* you are going about improving as much as *what* you are doing and how long you are doing it.

This is an *intense example of intensity,* but the point it this: if you want to become more confident as an athlete (or in any arena of life), you need to put the work in and you need to do it the right way. And if you want to become world-class, it will take a combination of natural skill, hard work, and *smart, evolutionary work.*

We are the ones who need to teach our athletes this idea and leave the ball in their court if they want to take it to the next level.

Coach Lesson #4: Performance Pillars

"To be unclear is to be unkind."
-CHRIS HOGAN

We must give our athletes a clearer roadmap to success.

Recently, I did a Mindset Coaching Session with an athlete named Carmen. Carmen was a freshman soccer player who wanted to make varsity. I asked him the question, "What's it going to take?"

His reply, "Hard work and dedication."

"Yep, that's not gonna cut it," I said to him.

"Everyone says that," I said. "Everyone *knows* that. All the other freshman who want to make varsity say that too. But can you tell me what exactly a varsity-level soccer player who has made the team and been successful actually does? His routines? What he focuses on? What he does differently?"

No, because Carmen's coach was unclear and therefore, is unkind. No coach or mentor had ever sat down with him and showed him the formula to discover what an actual "Five Steps to Make Varsity Game Plan" looked like. Kids are missing this kind of next level coaching guidance.

So we started breaking it down and came up with these five steps, in no particular order:

1. **Skills Development**

    a. Shooting

    b. Passing

    c. IQ/Reactivity

2. **Extreme Coachability**

    a. Ask the coach what exactly is needed to make the team and thrive

    b. Ask another player who has made varsity, "What should I work on? What does *this coach* look for?"

3. **Athleticism**

    a. Strength

    b. Speed

    c. Conditioning

4. **Strong Culture Fit**

    a. Enthusiastic

    b. Encouraging

    c. Positive attitude despite things not going your way

5. **Determined, Disciplined**

    a. No-quit mentality

    b. Shows up early to practice

    c. Attends all "extra" meetings/trainings/film

    d. Motivating work ethic for other players to see

Your Performance Pillars

If you are a coach that wants to field an all-star team, I suggest creating *your* 3-5 pillars or qualities that you look for in a player. Share this list with all prospective players at minimum six months before tryouts. Give them specific guidance and time to marinate on and take action on these things. Essentially, you are listing out your values and culture on paper. You are pre-qualifying players by clearly quantifying what it takes to make the team and thrive.

Letting the prospective players know very clearly what your expectations are is not only fair to the players for many reasons, but it will also make your team better, your job more enjoyable, and the results enhanced.

The 3-5 Pillars of Our Ideal Athlete

1. _____

2. _____

3. _____

4. _____

5. _____

Coach Lesson #5: Communicate to *Connect*

David Jacobson from the Positive Coaching Alliance says the number one problem he sees with most coaches is that they do not connect with their players.

"If you as a coach do not take into account your player's personality, their individuality, and their opportunity for development as a total person, you're blowing it. You are abdicating your responsibility as a coach for sports. You should be focused on character education and developing better athletes, better people."

Here are Three Simple-But-Not-Easy Ways to Connect with Your Athletes Better

1. Meet with each athlete individually twice per season at minimum.

Thirty minutes, one on one. Have specific questions for the athlete to answer *before* the meeting, along with some questions to ask during. This will create a culture where your athletes know you are always there for them.

"What is your biggest challenge or obstacle right now in this sport?"

"What is your biggest challenge or obstacle right now in life?"

"How can I best help you overcome those obstacles?"

"As your coach, how can I be a better leader for you?"

There are certainly other questions you can ask, but at the end of the day, those two 30-minute sessions could change that young man or woman's life. They could inspire them to believe in themselves. This is the impact we committed to making as coaches when we signed up.

2. Teach during non-conflict times.

I believe one of the reasons we are very successful at teaching our student-athletes life lessons is because we do it every day. We do not wait until they mess up or do something wrong to teach.

One way we teach during non-conflict times is that at the beginning of *every* workout session, one of our coaches facilitates an already planned mindset strengthening exercise. This exercise usually has a writing or interactive sharing component to go with it. Teaching life lessons needs to be part of your routine if you want to connect with your players better.

3. Be vulnerable.

Share your flaws, your weaknesses, and your heart. There is no better way to connect with another human than to make them realize you too are human.

If you take the time to better understand the psychology of your players, what is going on in their minds, and what they are feeling, then you can better prepare messages and stories that make them realize you too went through similar trials.

Athletes, especially middle and high schoolers, want to feel that they are understood. When you know that your coach understands you, that they "get you," you are more open to growing and changing. Do this one alone and it will lead to a higher performing team over time.

Coach Lesson # 6: Getting Athletes OUT Of Their Heads

Athletes in Their Heads

There was a section earlier to help the *athlete* get out of his or head and into the zone. I know it drives coaches and parents nuts when your athlete has the *ability* to perform one way but plays *beneath* that ability because they struggle with getting "in their own heads."

Why are they in their head?

There could be a number of reasons an athlete is in their head before competition. The key as a love-powered mindset coach is to recognize that an athlete's state of mind is their biggest threat *and* their biggest asset. It can literally make or break them.

- They could be nervous to go against that same team or competitor that beat them last time.

- They had a bad week of practice, they didn't train that week, or they were sick.

- They are overcoming an injury or the *fear* of a re-injury.

These are all common reasons. However the most common and easily fixable reason is because *we are in their head* – parents and coaches.

Pre-game and In-game Reminders

Pre- and in-game reminders increase the pressure an athlete feels, it leads them to fear disappointing you, and it frustrates them.

In a nutshell, they cause athletes to overthink, which we all know is the last thing you want to be doing as an athlete.

"Johnny, make sure to do what we practiced today. When you shoot, make sure you follow through. Don't fade away or off to the side. Now, go get 'em!"

Our intention is to help.

Inwardly, your athlete is most likely thinking, *"Dad/Mom is only going to be satisfied if I perform well. I can't mess up. I need to make sure I don't fade away. I want their praise and recognition."*

Outwardly, they may be showing or saying, *"Duh, I spend 15 hours a week practicing this. I don't need all of these reminders, especially right before a game!"*

And they are right. They do practice all the time. They have been playing the game for a while now. At practice is the time to remind them and reinforce the lessons, not games.

As the late John Wooden always reinforced, if you have done a great job as a coach, game time should be the time you sit back and watch the magic happen.

If you are reminding your players about the fundamentals *during the game*, you have not done a sufficient job reinforcing them during *practice*.

The "SAY NOTHING" Challenge

In the spring of 2019, we ran a challenge that went viral on social media. I was sick of hearing coaches and parents yell, pummel kids with reminders, say too much (thinking more was better), and ultimately lead athletes to frustration and burnout.

If you are a parent, I want you to try this. It is *guaranteed to* help your athletes play better. If you are a coach, there is a section below for you too. But even if you do not engage in the coach challenge, read the parent one. Every coach wants the parents off their backs and on their sides.

For two weeks for *all* games/matches/meets/competitions, *here* is the challenge:

o **No pre-game reminders.** This not only undermines your athlete's intelligence, but it also makes them overthink.

o **No bribes.** "Two bucks for every steal. Ten bucks for a every goal. McDonald's if you win. (I think that's more of a punishment, personally.)

o **No "I know you will do great" pregame comments.** This creates unneeded pressure to perform. "I gotta do great if I want to impress them."

o **No yelling during games.** Cheering is great, but we all know when it crosses over to criticizing or condemning coaches, referees, and even the athletes. Ask yourself, "If I was in their shoes, what would help me most from the fans?"

o **No sending your athlete motivational quotes or pump up speeches.** Let the coaches handle this.

o **No post-game mutism or post-game "game talk" (10-minute rule).** No changing your voice inflections, no getting weirdly quiet or overly talkative after games. Also, no talking about the game during the car ride.

KEEP IT SUPER SIMPLE, LOW STRESS, LOW PRESSURE.

Chances are, the stakes aren't that high anyway. Even if it is a conference or state championship, the long-term implications are minimal. Say nothing and watch what happens.

"My husband and I had no idea that we were causing our son so much stress and unneeded pressure before games. I knew I was loud during games, but I did not realize that he was getting in his own head BECAUSE of it! And after the games, I never knew what to say. This challenge has changed everything. He actually wants to talk after games now that I have disciplined myself to 'keep it simple.' This challenge could transform everything for your athlete, as well as your relationship with them."

-- PARENT WHO COMPLETED THE CHALLENGE

THE RESULTS OF FOLLOWING THE GUIDELINES BELOW:

1. Less overthinking, better performance

2. Less fear of making mistakes

3. Less fear of disappointing you, their teammates, their coaches

4. Less of a drop in self-esteem if they do perform poorly

5. Less of a jump in pride if they perform well

6. More joy, more enthusiasm, more excitement

PRE-GAME

"Good luck honey!"

"See you after the game!"

DURING GAME

Clap, cheer, converse with fellow parents. DO NOT SAY ANYTHING TO THE REFS! And of course, say *nothing* to your athlete while they are playing. This is the worst thing a parent can do. Your athlete will be embarrassed, in their head, and will play worse.

Tell other parents about the challenge and be the example!

POST-GAME

I want you to say the most powerful six words a parent could ever say to their kid after a game: *"I really love watching you play."*

And then, zip it. Let them talk or not talk. It doesn't matter. Just stop there.

I know by this point you may be cringing and experiencing a bit of anxiety. Your emotional investment in your kids play is well intended, but it is killing their confidence and having an adverse effect. Stay strong with this challenge. You and your spouse will likely giggle later on about how funny this was.

This is a proven way to help your kid play the best they possibly can and to help *you* enjoy the process of watching them during their sport.

If your athlete continues to experience fear and anxiety before games, or any other negative emotions pre- or post-performance, *you must try something different.*

Please accept this challenge and share it with others. You will not be disappointed. I believe in you. Your athletes deserve it.

Love-powered leaders choose to make changes in the way they do things, *especially when it is hard.*

A Challenge for Coaches

PRE-GAME

Most coaches fill their athletes' heads with tons of reminders, chalk talk, plays, and quite frankly, pressure-packed expectations.

Before your next game, look at your players and fill them with *confidence.*

"Fellas/Ladies, you've worked hard this week in practice. You are prepared. Expect to win but recognize you may fall short. I want you to give your best and let the refs and scoreboard take care of themselves. You've got this. I believe in you."

Simple, inspiring, to the point. This is something the greatest coaches do well. They are intentional about filling their team with confidence while at the same time not causing them extra fear or unneeded overthinking.

DURING THE GAME

Don't scream. When players are tired, all they hear is yelling. Plus they have to deal with the fans. And if they made a mistake, they are already having a loud conversation in their own head. They will not hear you. Your yelling will make it worse.

What *does* help, on the other hand, is calm, poised, collected reminders like:

"Move on, let that play go."

"Onward. Next play."

"You are still my guy. You are still my girl. You could mess up a million more times and you are still the guy/gal. Keep working hard."

Boom. Pressure released. Fear of getting benched released. Fear of disappointing coach released. I've surveyed over 1,000 athletes and 98.4% say they fear disappointing their team, parents, and coaches.

Focus on relieving your athletes of *fear* and they will play better. This goes back to *mindset coaching*. We try to address physical mistakes with physical reminders and new plays.

Missed a three-point shot? You need to jump higher next time!

Turned the ball over? You need to pass better next time!

Instead, try what I wrote about. Help them *forget about it and move on.* Do not freak out when your players mess up.

Freak-outs = fear-filled athletes.

There *is* a time to draw up plays and remind your players about the Xs and Os. But be intentional about *what they need most right then and there.* It is unlikely they are going to become a more skilled or physically gifted player in that moment of the game, right?

POST GAME

I've watched players get lectured for 45 minutes after a game. My guess is they heard the first, I don't know, five minutes? Attention spans are estimated at seven seconds as of 2019. So your athletes likely hear the first seven seconds, then they checkout for 10-15 seconds. Then they come back for another seven. By the time you get to five minutes, they are *gone*.

Their blood glucose is depleted from their brains after a long game. Have *you* ever tried to focus after a workout, before getting food? Physiologically, it is not really possible.

Keep the post-game wrap-up quick. But always have an *intended outcome.* Your goal should not be for your athletes to leave fearful of what you are going to do to them at practice. That is coercive power and a big mistake if you care about your relationship with your players.

A love-powered outcome would be to leave them feeling inspired and excited to get better. Whether they won or lost, had a great game or terrible one, you want them to look forward to practice the next day. You want them to look forward to the next game. Of course, you want them to *learn something* from that game, but that learning should take place the next day.

Keep it short and simple. Let them go home, eat, and live their lives. Besides, isn't the goal to teach them life lessons? If you have a bad day at work, isn't the goal to leave that bad day *at work* and to go home and enjoy your evening with your family? Monkey see, monkey do. Teach your kids the keys to a great life and remember that it is *just a game.*

Anything can be taught, but not everything is worth teaching

We just spent a good chunk of time going through these practical lessons. If you do not continue to train *your* mental game, you will quickly head back into the rat race of, "how do I get my players to play better."

You can learn anything as a coach, and you can teach your players *anything you want*. There are so many things we can choose to spend our time getting better at. That is a blessing, but also a trap.

I'll ask you once more, what matters most? The values exercise *is* by far the most important one to revisit over and over again. It is the one your kids need to over and over again. Our values discrepancy *is* at the root of most evil. But on the contrary, something beautiful happens when we focus on the right stuff.

When we begin to shift our attention towards the things and the people in our lives that matter most, the stars begin to align.

I want to close with my favorite story of all time, one that you would be wise to share with your players, your kids, and your students. Lord knows we need more love-powered coaches who lead with *this* philosophy.

Coach Lesson #7: The Cup, the Sleeve, the Napkin

When you go to a coffee shop, the only thing you are thinking about is that cup of coffee – the delicious, hot, strong, caffeinated cup of joe.

I mean honestly, who actively thinks about *not* burning their hand? No one, because we have the sleeve. The function of the sleeve is to cover the cup of coffee and protect you from burning your hand.

Without the sleeve, the cup of coffee is more of a burden than a pleasure. The cup of coffee is useless without the sleeve. If the sleeve wasn't around, the barista would have to make the coffee colder, which would make it far less enjoyable. No one wants lukewarm coffee. Therefore, I think we can all agree that the sleeve and the cup of coffee are equally important.

Moving on, have you ever *spilled* your coffee?

I remember months ago I was getting my holiday Starbucks cup of coffee, and as the barista was handing it to me, it shook in her hand just enough to spill over the edge of the cup where my hand was.

Thank goodness for the *napkin* that she had wrapped the cup in to accompany the coffee.

Napkins are there to clean up the millions of coffee spills that happen in coffee shops all over the world daily. If napkins ceased to exist, there would be a lot of problems. If Starbucks decided not to carry napkins anymore because they were not as *highly desired as a cup of coffee,* Starbucks would be a sticky, brown, dirty place.

The cup, the sleeve, and the napkin illustrate a critical life lesson for youth and for people in general.

Your sports team would be awful if all you had were cups.

Scorers. Highlight reel athletes. Stat builders. Who would play defense? Who would be the encouragers? Who would be the master assisters and passers? Who would be the one to clean up the shot that bounced off the post or crossbar by hustling to the net to follow up the scorer's shot?

We have placed such a premium on the cup that no one really *wants* to be the sleeve or the napkin, and that is just sad. We all have a responsibility to be napkins and sleeves at some point. We need to teach our athletes how important those two roles are by *recognizing and rewarding* the napkins and the sleeves.

Matthew 20:26 – Not so with you. Instead, whoever wants to become great among you must be your servant.

These are famous words from Jesus. His leadership example is one of the reasons I follow His teachings so closely. The guy took twelve *below-average men* and built a dream team that changed the world. Billions of people now follow Him because his example of love-powered servant-leadership was so attractive. He knew the importance of being a cup, a sleeve, *and* a napkin.

I think this lesson applies to me as much as it does the athletes I coach. I need to be the ultimate example of a willing, excited sleeve and napkin. I need to show my athletes that the cup of coffee is part of the team – it is not *the team*. I need to led like Jesus led. I need to be a servant to my players.

"Whoever wants to be great among you must be your servant." As coaches, we *are* greater. We are wiser, stronger, and more capable. We have life experiences, failures, and successes to share. Therefore, because we *are* greater, we must serve these kids like we are working *for them*. Just as the "greater" parent changes the diaper and feeds the *less capable* baby, we too must serve our students wholeheartedly. That beautiful example will be one that echoes for generations to come. I believe that servant-leadership is the *only leadership*.

Love-powered coaches, will you join me in this movement?

CONCLUSION

As I mentioned, if you go to www.andrewjsimpson.com/book-insider you will find and can steal all of the practical exercises. The coaching shift you decide to make after reading this book will help your athletes level up in the dimensions of their lives that are being neglected.

Every week, you should be objectively assessing the state of your athletes minds and hearts. "What is their vibrancy like? How excited are they? How much joy and enthusiasm are they bringing to what they do each day?"

As a coach, what is my objective? What do I want my legacy to be about?

For me, it is clear. I am on a mission to help millions of coaches, parents, and athletes realize their full God-given potential and become more confident, successful leaders in sports and life.

I spend my time and money on things that support that mission. If an opportunity pops up that does not align with that or will take time and money away from it, I say no to it, no matter how great the opportunity.

The resources you now have access to at the website have helped thousands of student-athletes and coaches to escape the norm and become the 1%, the 1% of those who experience joy, enthusiasm, and peak performance. Mindset solutions exist, and now you can deliver them.

Thank you for taking the time to read this book. Do the writing exercises. But most importantly, keep learning. Do not become the old dog that refuses to learn new tricks.

As Jesus said at the Sermon on the Mount in Matthew 7:7-8, "Ask and it will be given to you; *seek and you will find*; knock and the door will be opened to you. For everyone who asks receives; *the one who seeks finds*; and to the one who knocks, the door will be opened."

Seek to become the best coach you can be. Focus less on how to win or get more out of your athletes (the fruit) and more on becoming a better coach (the root). You will change the lives of millions, just as we are on a mission to do. We are in this together.

ABOUT THE AUTHOR

One Decision Changed My Life

It wasn't until I was 19 years old that I finally started becoming Andrew Simpson. Up until that point, I was a follower and didn't even know it.

At age 19 I found a mentor who changed the trajectory of my life. All I needed was a new path, and I found it. The Law of the Path states that the path you are on *will* take you to the destination that that path leads to. Finally, I stepped onto the right one.

But nights were lonely. I left my friend group of 13 years, stopped the things I needed to stop, and started the things I knew I needed to start doing.

I wanted to spend more time reading books and learning how to be a better leader, how to be more confident, resilient, helpful, and successful. I wanted to spend time around other people who shared my interests. My friends did not. That is what an influential mentor can do. He or she can take a 19-year-old party kid and transform his mindset overnight.

What was the result? For more than a year I spent Friday and Saturday nights hanging out with mom and pops. It wasn't the coolest thing I had ever done, but it was worth it.

Because just two years later by age 21, God was starting to put people in my life whom I was called to coach and positively impact. I was helping student-athletes, my peers, and even adults! I was using what I learned and what was helping *me* to help *others*.

People were beginning to say, "There is something different about Andrew." I tell our athletes all the time, "That is what you want to hear others saying behind your back. There is something different about _____ (insert your name)."

Finally a few years later, I had set myself up to open a business at 24 years old with a team of people who were more like me than any group of people I had ever hung around. In some ways they were like me, but in other ways they were uniquely themselves, which is awesome.

Tough Decisions Lead to Big Rewards

If not for that decision to leave my friend group and change my life at age 19, I may not have ever gone to Salisbury University, which was a recommendation from somebody who I only met because I stopped wasting my nights hanging out playing video games in my friends basement, and instead started working at a sports complex at night.

If I had never gone to Salisbury, I would not have gotten my degree in Exercise Science, which allowed me to become a better personal trainer and strength coach.

I also would have never met my wife! Her name is Daniela DeMarco Simpson. She is an Italian and she is beautiful, both inside and out. I married up, big time. She took a chance on me, hopefully one that she now would say has paid off.

And had I *not* made that definitive decision to change my ways, the following event would not have taken place…

On January 3, 2019 our son was born. God brought Jack Joseph Simpson into our world just seven weeks after my dad had gone home to Him. Just as He promises us, He wiped the tears of sadness away from our eyes and replaced them with tears of joy.

Was it worth it?

If I had not made the decision I made at 19, I may have never decided to go to FCF church. I learned about who God *really* was and ended up developing a relationship with Him (which is something I didn't even know you could do before that).

I learned about who Jesus was, how He walked this earth and for three years taught people how to live well. How he was the perfect Servant-Leader. He took twelve dudes who were anything but extraordinary, turned them into *leaders*, and inspired and influenced them to go out and change the world. He demonstrated His servant's heart by washing their feet, even though he was the leader!

If I never made the decision to be a thermostat and live my truth, I would not have had the opportunity to baptize my dad three months before he died.

Because of one "small" decision I made at 19 years old to be myself and stop following the crowd, I learned *everything I know* about how to be a great leader.

You can inspire your athletes to make big decisions today.

I am not who I was 10 years ago at age 19, and I am not the man today that I will be at age 39. At least I really hope not. I want to be better. I want to strengthen my discernment muscle so I know when something is my will versus God's. I want to continue to shed away my impatient attitude, my overworking syndrome, and my other character flaws that remind me I'll always need a Savior. I want to *allow* for more peace and contentment in my life, I am not the best at slowing down. Like Paul, I start to slow down, then I just fall back into the same trap.

I really want to be better at inspiring others to live the life God created them for. This is going to take better communication and love on my part. I know He can do more through me if I work diligently, trust Him completely, and consecrate *everything in my life* to Him. I mean come on, He turned a few pieces of bread and fish into enough to feed 5000 people.

How much can He do through you and I if we give him our businesses, our finances, our influence, our athletes, our gameplan, our families, and our entire lives? One decision - I guarantee you will not be disappointed.

ACKNOWLEDGEMENTS

Ifirst want to acknowledge my selfless, loving wife, Daniela. Thank you for allowing me to (attempt to) hang up shelves for you in your college apartment back in 2011. For being my *biggest* supporter. For your countless sacrifices over the past decade to support the mission God has given me. Jack has won the lottery with you as his mother. I don't tell you this enough, but you *are* my angel. I love you.

To my family: Mom, Cass, and Julia. You three are a big part of my *why*. Your strength, your endurance, and your love has encouraged me to press on during the times I have felt like quitting. Mom, thank you for starting this family and showing us through example that the person in front of you is most important. Dad would be thrilled to see where you are at in life right now. Thank you for showing me how to be a good listener, how to forgive, and how to love. Cass and Julia, you two are the definition of perseverance. I am so grateful for the never-ending, unconditional support you show me. You both amaze me and make me want to be better. I love you three so much.

To the PFP Team. You may not realize this but writing this book would not have been possible without you. Steph, Daniela, Kelsey, Rachel, Joe, Brian, Travis, Tanya, Erik, Julia, Cathy, Chris, and Ben. Your love for our mission, your servant-hearts, and your daily sacrifices allowed me the time and opportunity to write The Youth Truth. We are on this journey together and believe me, it is just getting started.

Tanya, thank you for believing in this mission from the start, for "bull-horning" it to the world, and being the "beta tester" for our sports parent principles and best practices. You've inspired me to be a better relationship builder, a better question asker, a better hugger, and to love people unconditionally.

Travis, thank you for loving our student-athletes with all your heart and for caring so deeply about the integrity and success of our coaches and the program. Because of you and our amazing coaches, I was able to write this book knowing the "root" was more than taken care of.

To Todd Durkin. I want you to know that you turned PFP from a business idea into a crusade. In 2014, I was directionless. I knew I needed help. God sent me to San Diego to learn from one of His faithful servants. You delivered. I could not imagine my life, my family, or my business without your influence. Thank you for modeling servant leadership and for showing me what it means to stay true to your values no matter what. And finally, thank you for sending my dad thoughtful videos when he needed them the most. Your commitment to being present and available may be the quality I admire most about you. You have made a *generational impact* over here, TD.

To the countless mentors I have been blessed to learn from. My pastors, Randy and Thomas, for speaking spiritual truth into my life and teaching me what it *really* means to follow Jesus. To Dave Ramsey, for teaching me how to cast vision and run a business congruent with Biblical values. And to the many others who have counseled me and given me wisdom at pivotal times in my life.

Last but not least, to the loyal PFP Guests. For trusting us. For giving my life purpose. You have brought so much joy to our lives. You have stuck by our side during growing pains and have trusted us to always do the right thing for you. Thank you for your support, your encouragement, and your belief in us.

Made in the USA
Middletown, DE
26 July 2021

44786877R00191